The Soul of Startups

The Soul of Startups

The Untold Stories of How Founders Affect Culture

Sophie Theen

WILEY

Published by John Wiley & Sons, Inc., Hoboken, New Jersey.
Published simultaneously in Canada.

For general information on our other products and services or for technical support, please contact our Customer Care Department within the United States at (800) 762-2974, outside the United States at (317) 572-3993 or fax (317) 572-4002.

Wiley also publishes its books in a variety of electronic formats. Some content that appears in print may not be available in electronic formats. For more information about Wiley products, visit our web site at `www.wiley.com`.

Library of Congress Cataloging-in-Publication Data is Available:

ISBN 9781119885597 (hardback)
ISBN 9781119885610 (ePDF)
ISBN 9781119885603 (ePub)

Cover Design: Wiley
Cover Image: © Ekaterina Bedoeva/Getty Images

Printed and bound by CPI Group (UK) Ltd, Croydon, CR0 4YY

C003843_060722

To those who inspired it,

Good and Bad.

Thank you for setting me free.

Contents

Foreword   ix

Preface   xiii

Introduction   1

CHAPTER 1   The Gen Z Leader   7

CHAPTER 2   The Type A   21

CHAPTER 3   The Talent Acquirer   43

CHAPTER 4   The Middle Manager   65

CHAPTER 5   The Unlearner   77

CHAPTER 6   The Trailblazer   95

CHAPTER 7   The Collectivist versus The Individualist   115

CHAPTER 8   The Community Builder   135

CHAPTER 9   The Keen Learner   157

CHAPTER 10   The Black Diamond   177

Closing Reflections   203

Acknowledgments   209

About the Author   211

Index   213

Foreword

"It really is *that* simple." I stood nodding my head under drizzling rain in the middle of Hyde Park, re-reading my WhatsApp exchange with Sophie. "Mental bookmark," I said aloud and continued walking. She and I had been going back-and-forth about a particularly stressful interpersonal work conundrum I was experiencing, and I was in search of some tough love wrapped in sympathy, which is exactly what I got.

For most of my career, particularly the last decade, I've been pursuing a vision of work where I feel confident, valued, and fulfilled. Why is that remarkable in any way? It's not. We're all doing the same thing, every day. However, it *is* remarkable to find someone who challenges and helps you refine your thinking to make both your pursuit *and* your vision not only sensible but attainable. Even more remarkable is finding someone with whom to build that vision. I (and many others) found that person in Sophie. Together, she and I have spent countless hours bonding over our shared passions, similarities, differences and, ultimately, how we want to make changes in the world.

Sophie and I first met in person in December 2019 in the London HQ of the FinTech company she had recently joined. I was in the recruitment process to join and was looking to leave my role at a large, very stable organisation, to head up marketing and customer acquisition at this much smaller B2C FinTech. I had ambitious plans to seriously disrupt traditional consumer lending. I arrived in a suit. Sophie turned up with rainbow hair, workout pants, and sneakers. "Cooooooooool," I smiled as she opened the door of the soundproof meeting room pod.

One of the first things you notice about Sophie is that she knows her stuff. She can get down to business in a way that makes you confident she is *handling* whatever she's handling. The second, third, and fourth things might be her brightly dyed hair, her tattoos, and/or that she is physically very, very small. Immediately, I wanted to know her MBTI type. A dated reference? Maybe. Nonetheless, I really wanted to know!

That day, we ended up chatting about a worrying new SARS-like virus that we'd been hearing about, handwashing (why doesn't everybody just do it already?), social trust in Asian cities versus European ones, and lots of other seemingly random topics. I say "seemingly random" because when we were done, she closed the conversation by summarising her takeaways against the points and questions she had had regarding my candidacy. Clever! That was *my* trick—get to know someone quickly and relatively profoundly through active listening and lots of specific yet casual questions. Now I *really* wanted to know this Sophie woman.

In the end, I accepted the role of Chief Marketing Officer, which morphed into Chief Product & Marketing Officer and, finally, into Chief Executive Officer over my tenure with the firm. Along the way, Sophie and I formed a decisive allyship and friendship, nourished by direct and honest conversation and a lot of shared values, two of which repeatedly make their way to the forefront of our discussions: 1) leading by example with compassion and empathy, and 2) leaving a team, department, company, industry, or all the above better than you found it.

I started the CMO role on the 18th of March 2020, a date I will not soon forget. COVID-19 was surging (for the first time) in the UK and the entire country was placed under lockdown the very next day. Over the nearly two years that followed, I was fortunate to work closely with Sophie and benefit from her well-worn experience navigating an incredibly broad range of subjects and personalities. At the same time, she—like everyone else—was learning how to lead in a pandemic, being faced with new demands and circumstances every week if not every day. It is plain to see why Sophie has chosen the unpredictable and exhilarating world of startups. She is simply brilliant under these circumstances.

At a time when the entire world was in upheaval, no one knew exactly what to do, which sounds unbelievable but was 100 percent the case. Governments were enacting then reversing then updating mandates every couple of days in an attempt to get in front of the pandemic while not crippling their economies. Streets emptied almost overnight. Businesses shuttered. "Fortunate" employees flicked on their computers at home instead of at the office, and for the most part kept grinding. Of many, the notable exception was, of course, parents whose lives descended into chaos that needed specific and urgent support from employers. For the less fortunate, however, work was severely disrupted—some of which will never return to pre-pandemic conditions.

For most of 2020, navigating legislation around furloughing, employment status, and place of work was nothing short of a nightmare. But when the going gets tough, the tough get going. And the truly brilliant get to bettering. Enter Sophie.

Certainly, Sophie is intelligent and incredibly skilled at her craft. She is meticulous, efficient, and an unbelievably hard worker. But it is her regard for others that makes her a cut above. Many teammates and employees will never know the extent to which she has gone for them. Over the course of our working together, she has (sometimes angrily) called me many, many times with the same question, "Is this the best we can do for this employee?"

Fellow reader, in this book, you will dive into FinTech startups from a unique and rare point of view. No, not that of the serial entrepreneur or the battle-weary VC but that of a compassionate leader who, in my experience, is one of the most clutch players on a startup executive team—the person in charge of people. What does it mean to be in charge of people at an early to early-ish-stage FinTech venture? Read on.

I was overjoyed when I heard that Sophie was penning a book. In these pages, you will not only find the story of how she and, thus, her career took off, but also a view behind her decision-making and a unique and admirably straightforward methodology for understanding, digesting, and then weaponizing professional experiences (the good, the bad, and the traumatic). Known for speaking and acting very purposefully, Sophie isn't one to flaunt what she knows. She's more like a quiet precision tool that never stops working. But as Stephen Hawking famously said, "Quiet people have the loudest minds." And now her mind to a large extent, but more importantly her learnings, are captured here and shared with you. Enjoy.

Amber Skinner-Jozefson,
Startup Advisor,
London

Preface

In the middle of the pandemic when the world was turned upside down overnight, some of us out there were still consumed by the notoriety of startup behaviors while most of us were mourning the loss of freedom, a social life, families, and friends. I thought to myself, surely people stuck at home don't need to read more about who's done what wrong to who, but I was clearly naïve. I was still getting calls from journalists asking if I could comment on why Revolut was yet again being seen as a malicious employer. So, I picked up a pen (yes, physically at first) and started to write down my answers to their questions.

It began to look like a long overdue angered letter by a bitter ex-employee who might have felt they had missed out on riding the waves of something bigger than a unicorn. But the more I wrote, the more I realized, that I too was at fault. I circled at my own behaviors, my misperceptions, the allowances I made as excuses for poor behaviors of leaders that continued to encourage their disrepute. I was half the problem.

This book is about the journeys of startup operators in both the good and bad forms. Some have had the luxury of being in healthy, thriving environments but I credit this to their ability to set boundaries for both themselves and their leaders. They clearly knew what they were doing, what fitted them, and not because they were lucky. I sadly did not learn this until after I survived a train crash in this ecosystem. Since then, I have continued to learn from my mistakes (I genuinely hope you will, too) and was able to stay a mile away from those who aren't suited for what is needed.

Founders are the leaders who started the companies, but let's be honest, they are not and will not build their businesses all by themselves. They need their people, they need us. So, while historically we may spend the day glorifying these successful, magnificent super-heroes, I want you to spend equally the same time celebrating those who worked alongside them, turned problems into solutions, hiring multitudes of talent even when CEOs scare them off, and probably working in one of the hardest jobs they ever found themselves in. Because god forbid, journalists will do that for them right?

Another reason you'll not hear it directly from founders in this book is because we have more than enough platforms out there for founders to sugar-coat their company's existence and the culture they are building. If this book is meant to serve aspiring founders, opera-tors, and perhaps investors too with some truth, then they need to hear it from the people who lived through it firsthand, with absolutely no filters.

Know that I'm writing this from a People (HR [human resources]) perspective who reports to the CEO and is there to, "Build this culture with me" so my experiences are drawn from working closely with them so that I understand the psychology that shaped the personal-ities and behaviors you see. At the same time, my generous inter-viewees either share my profile or have experienced these cultures after they are "built."

As you start reading this, I remind you that this isn't about blam-ing founders who hadn't done the right thing or weren't experienced enough to build the company that was good for its people. It isn't meant to bring shame to the wrongdoings, but to provide insight on how it affects the people working for them. Founders are human too, and we should unequivocally cut them some slack if we knew they hadn't built a company before. However, at what point does it turn into excuses, is a question I hope you will continue to ask yourself.

And this is why I've called this, *The Soul of Startups*, because it all starts from the Founder.

Introduction

A workplace environment that values creative problem solving, open communication, and a flat hierarchy is popularly defined as a **startup culture**. Typically, in a **corporate culture**, the core values are communicated through a mission statement, products, and customer needs.

When it comes to startups, this statement couldn't be further from the truth. In the beginning, a startup company is scrappy, disorganized, and going through headcount stages that start at 1 and skyrocket to 5,000. Due to this rapid growth, the culture has no choice other than evolve from a business that's required to claw to a full-blown hierarchical structure. This change is implemented to sustain the growth.

In this book, we will dive into the many stages of a startup company and watch how the culture has matured in the best and worst ways. I am going to take this moment to remind everyone reading that this is not a "how to" book. In these pages you will find a compilation of activities I've witnessed and situations I've experienced. Each one is like a tattoo or scar.

My hope is to leave you with a shortcut to immerse yourself into the startup culture. While reading you will learn from my joy and pain but then come to the end making up your own mind.

A BIT ABOUT ME

Reflecting on the past has never been my style. When trauma reared its ugly head, I was always the type of person who would blow past it and carry on with my life. In my mind I could hear myself say, "That experience can never hurt me again because now I know better."

Yet, then when I found myself in the startup world everything was different, including the people. I was unable to predict what was going to happen in this strange, unstable environment. When I would hear a colleague holler, "I don't care about what they think, just get rid of them if they can't get on board!" day in and day out as the phrase was repeated, my soul would cringe.

I learned the hard way and found I was disappointed in my company and in myself, for allowing things like that to happen. As an HR professional I care about the people I work with and my heart wasn't into this type of practice.

MY JOURNEY

When they handed me my diploma, the global financial crisis was well underway, which meant finding a permanent position was out of the equation for me. Yet, I held out and an opportunity came knocking on my door as I joined a particular startup as their first tech recruiter.

This startup was my destiny, even if I didn't realize it right away. After a while I did understand that I was meant to be in the startup business because it fit me and my character to a tee. Little did I know I was going to play a significant role in shaping what we now call Startup Culture.

After a year of working with this startup I found that I struggled but I loved every moment of it. I didn't know what a valuable experience this was, but I would soon find out. I didn't make much money compared to my peers whom I graduated with, and I would feel embarrassed to discuss my work with them. I worked hard but didn't have anything to show for it.

One night I was meeting with my college friends, and I knew they would be talking about their jobs. I feared they would ask me "How's your work? Did you learn anything new?" These people were working for large corporations or rotating in graduate programs. My standard answer was, "It's okay. Nothing new." That couldn't have been further from the truth.

The fact was I was learning something new every day. I was working with a small team of three, my CEO was hands-on and willing to coach me to develop the skills I have today. For some reason, I still felt ashamed when I saw the glances of judgement when I told my friends I took a job as a recruiter, a career they didn't want so they questioned why I would follow that path.

When I was at work, I was cold calling, yet I hardly made a commission. What I was doing was learning. I received an education in a whole new industry that my four years of college didn't prepare me for. Even when things were going well, and we were successful I was still ashamed to talk about my work. I thought I wasn't part of a huge corporation that would stand out on my CV for the rest of my career.

After sticking it out for two years I figured, "I know what I'm doing. It's time to get a job with a corporation. One that would bring me a safer feeling than the stress that comes with thinking about a runaway company." I wanted job security that was promised with a large company. Even if it meant taking a pay cut in the long run, it was what I needed to secure a mortgage.

These were my personal circumstances, and I was fortunate enough to walk right into it. There I was finally at ease and had a feeling of contentment for six months.

What I wasn't aware of were the office politics and the bureaucracy I saw around me. I was told I might be promoted if I just stayed in the same job for the next 12 months, but it was up to the "company's discretion." What did this all mean? After some soul-searching it finally hit me. Autonomy was my drive back in the day. I loved "being part of the journey," which is what the early stages of a startup offers.

Still, I couldn't walk away. I was 25 and a mere signature away from buying my first home. How could I leave now? The answer was, I couldn't. So, I stayed for the next four years and kept a journal of the lessons I learned. I kept myself safe behind a shield I constructed so I could climb the corporate ladder utilising the same tools I learned from them. Use their expertize against them per se.

Corporate Life is riddled with politics and a bureaucratic mentality that would shock some. The secrecy behind it all was especially staggering. Still, I sacrificed my principles because I was settling down with a career (so I thought), and it wasn't a good time to give up my security.

FINALLY GETTING STARTED

In 2016, the word FinTech started to pop up all over the place. I thought it was a sexy word being described as "financial services in hoodies." When I heard about it, I was intrigued. More importantly, I had just moved across the pond and was living in London after my relationship broke down. I was definitely ready and in need of a change.

Change came calling for me on a damp April evening at 7:30 p.m. I was waiting for an interview outside a small office in Canary Wharf and was surprised to see how at least 80 percent of the seats were still occupied by employees. Especially at that hour. Each desk occupant was focused on their dual screens while I waited around for another 20 minutes for the CEO, who had already delayed our interview by an hour.

Once I was in his office, he offered me a glass of water, shook my hand, and went straight into it.

"Tell me what added value you can bring to my company?" was the first question he asked me.

He didn't want to waste time if I waffled on about my starting journey as a struggling graduate. He wasn't interested in how I got there that evening. He wanted to know why I was the right person for the job.

I felt a tingle. The good kind. It was a feeling I remember from 2011 when Kevin, the CEO, told me I was going to be better off being a recruiter in his startup than holding out for a graduate engineer job that may or may not happen anytime soon.

"Is this the sign I've been waiting for?" is a question I played over and over in my head during the interview.

I lit up and told him, "I know how to do this job. I've already had one, and I've been doing this exact same thing for the last few years. Unfortunately, none of my efforts were enough for my manager to see that I deserved a promotion. So, I'm going to find that promotion elsewhere. I hope that it's here."

He thanked me for coming in and explained that he needed to go back into another meeting. Before he walked away, he offered me the job on the spot. I was going to be the Global Head of HR for Revolut. It was the start of a whirlwind career path that brought me adventures and joy that I wouldn't trade for anything. Especially when I look back at that first day.

Fast forward six years, and I've been a part of 11 startups and the number keeps rising. I've seen the good and the bad, the devils and angels in the making, and I've felt the love and pain this ecosystem has given me. Now, it's time for me to break out my little black book of stories to tell you what you need to know about the truths of being here.

What I had to sacrifice, what I learned could never bring me down in life, and the joy I got through this journey I couldn't have experienced elsewhere, especially not in the corporate world.

This story is dedicated to those who feel startups are their destiny. Your destiny is calling.

What is important for you to realize is that I am telling you my story from the perspective of an HR person, not the founder. So, this shouldn't be used as a playbook for someone who is looking to hear about success stories. I am writing this for the person who wants to run a better people-centric company. This book will explain what you should and shouldn't do to people you call your employees.

I am also writing this book for everyday people who are curious about the startup world but aren't ready to sacrifice their job security at the moment. This is my secret diary that I am choosing to share with the world, and you. Some of you may get behind it and others might get defensive, but that's okay.

I'm not here to tell you that my perception is right and yours is wrong. If you don't agree then we are just two people who journeyed through life down a different path.

CHAPTER 1

The Gen Z Leader

THE FOUNDER CULTURE

The term "startup" is a term used quite loosely in today's society. Individuals ask, "What exactly is a startup?" and "What are specific types of startups?" Over time, I have come up with a simple answer. A startup is a novel business that aims to create a service or product that can be somewhat seamlessly scalable. The goal is to develop larger profit margins.

A startup product or service should aim to fix an issue in the market and fill a critical need. You could even create a new market entirely, which is the beauty of startups. These businesses achieve a lot of growth and can be transformative in five years or less, which is appealing to someone interested in starting a business.

One misconception people seem to have is that startups have to be in the tech industry. This misunderstanding is not valid. However, a large portion of them are, so it's understandable people would think this way. Startups that aren't software-based tend to have physical services or products that require economical solutions for creation.

Creating a company typically involves one individual or a group of people. These people are "founders." In the beginning, they have a vision of what they think that company can be. It is that vision that helps create the organisation's culture. In some instances, the founder, or founders, are highly intentional about developing a particular culture. One example is a business where teamwork or innovation is valued. On the other side, there are situations where the founder, or the most assertive personality in the group, inadvertently develops the culture from that base.

Some founders, or the core group, create buzz around their startup's culture even in the early stages when they have as little as five employees. A natural phenomenon in the startup world is when the founders become incredibly proud of the job they've done and what they were able to establish. But, as the startup grows and expands, they become stuck in a loop where their voice is the only one that makes sense.

When first starting, having a vocal founder can impact the culture positively, but it can soon become a poisoned chalice. At what point does their culture break?

THE GEN Z PARADIGM

Who Are They?

Technically, this is a term used for Generation Y. But I feel we attribute these traits to the wrong generation. The founders I spoke of are more characteristic of Gen Z. The youngest generation expects more innovation because they've grown up in an age of rapid modernization, which means they are hardly realistic and rarely focused on experience.

Some of the fastest-growing startups were born out of these generations. We must note that there are always horror stories lingering under the hood in every good story.

What is the story here?

Diversity means the practice of involving or including different voices and opinions, which is difficult to achieve when one voice stands out over them all. A founder who only hears his voice makes it difficult to build a diverse culture. What we do in the workplace should involve everyone's voice, which would lead to making justifiable decisions that would shape the very culture of a company.

"Oh, David? Do you mean the guy who interviewed you last month? He left the company. He was let go. It just wasn't the right role for him. He lacked courage."

That type of dialogue is a red flag. When Callum said that to me on my first day, the first thing I thought was, "Well, too bad for that guy." I didn't realize that it would be "too bad for me" six months later.

The keyword in his statement was "courage." In most situations, particularly HR, challenging the status quo is something we would never do. Our role in HR is the "guardian" of the company. Yet, with this new opportunity, I needed the courage to be the "betrayer" of all the other employees. I had to create false protection to ensure the business wasn't going to be sued left, right, and center.

Yet, I spent the majority of my next six months working through settlements as a means to justify my existence. This backtracking was my way to add value to this business or at least recognize what the role indeed was.

You see, David was a well-established HR leader in the industry and a person I felt I could learn from while working together. He had interviewed me only a month earlier after being with the startup for only two months. I admit I thought he wasn't successful in this business because he wasn't fast-paced or creative enough to bring HR into a new age.

When Callum "casually" interviewed me to be David's replacement, he made it clear that he wasn't interested in a traditional HR professional. The role he described required the person to make new frameworks like salary transparency and create other new ways to develop his original and fresh employees.

While many other startups fail, I felt I was sitting in front of a visionary CEO who believed I could bring the change he wanted that suited all of his employees. In the eight years I put into my career until that point, this was the first time I had been wrong about my soon-to-be manager. By the time I came on board, they had already gone through four HR directors in three short years. I may not have heard the sirens then, but my ears would perk up soon.

My first week went like this.

"I've heard so much about you, Sophie. I'm excited we'll be working together," was what the Chief of Staff said when meeting me and quickly moving into, "But first things first. I have an update; your manager Stephen (Chief Operating Officer) resigned a few weeks ago, so we're going to need you to be in Los Angeles to spend some hand-over time with him." She continued without stopping. "You'll be reporting to Callum from now on, and I'm here to support you in any way you need. But don't worry, we've started the process to hire a counterpart for you so that we don't have to bother regions covered. Come, shall we get a coffee and introduce you to the rest of the team?"

From there, she explained all the changes that had taken place over the last three months, which I first met with Callum. I couldn't help but feel a little giddy about this future. Still, something didn't sit right in my gut. But it was a new environment, a new industry, so I thought to myself, "I just need to be patient to see how this pans out." After all, everyone I met seemed "normal."

The next thing you know, I'm in LA, looking outside from a meeting room decked out with cushions, skateboards, and a slushie machine. Stephen, who was supposed to be my manager, walked in and said, "I hope you're enjoying the lovely weather but let's get to it. I should be out by the end of the week, so we only have five days to get through all the materials I have."

Contrary to what they told me on my first day, I didn't have a month's handover; it would last less than seven days. Since I was already used to the scrappy startup environment, I held my chin up and cracked on. This setback was just the beginning of events that would start to unravel as the months moved on because I was not in a real-life "one-man show."

So, let's do a quick recap.

In the three months I had been with the company, they fired David, Stephen resigned, and I was required to take care of a handover that needed a month in less than a week. Did I see the red flags yet? No, but my eyesight grew better in week two.

RED FLAG #1 (WEEK TWO)

"Just to catch you up on a few things," the in-house counsel said as she welcomed me. "We have two open cases that need your attention. I'm so glad you're here. We haven't had any HR counsel for a while, so they are stacking up."

"What do you mean?" I asked. "These cases look like my predecessor filed these more than a year ago. Didn't David look into them and come to a resolution?"

"Well, you see," she started to respond. "David was only here for a few months, and during that time, he didn't have any UK legislation experience or knowledge. So, they got passed on to the CFO, then COO, and then finally the Chief of Staff. Now it sits with you." Her smile was almost gratifying.

My brain immediately went into overdrive. What about the non-existence of management consequences in this company? If it didn't bother them at all, having it passed around to people who have no prior knowledge on how employment legislation worked. It put a dent in my confidence in their ability to delegate work appropriately. However, I was still in my second week. I am called "the fixer" for a reason, and here I was fixing the first problem.

(Week Three)

I stepped into a meeting scheduled to last 90 minutes that would begin upon my arrival. It was a small group consisting of executives and me. Callum gave me a heads up before the call, "If you can join, please, I'd like to observe and push back on unnecessary training needs if it is not at all mandatory by law."

Upon hearing this, I felt a surge of excitement. I was three weeks in, and it usually doesn't take this long after joining a new role but, I finally understood why I was here. My purpose would be to take the lead on what mattered to the people. The reason they hired me.

The meeting started like this.

"Change of plans. We will not pursue setting up a harassment workshop because I believe that we do not need to set the precedent of creating red tape in the company. We are a startup with the ability to chop and change our policies and can move faster this way so let's not start with training, policies, and rules that will stop us from having fun in our careers."

I nodded and said, "Sounds like a plan," and nothing more. These executives were the same ones involved with decision-making calls and passing tribunal cases around like a ball.

If it wasn't obvious yet, at that point, they threw me into the dark without any context whatsoever. What I did find out from the in-house counsel, not long after this meeting, was that the company already had a few harassment allegations against a senior manager in the inconclusive investigation. Upper management brought no consequences against the manager, and they told the alleged victim the same.

Not only was he not reprimanded for the first instance, but they also created a "no tolerance" policy that was also created almost directly after David filed this case. Which meant the senior manager would now walk free with a slap on his wrist. Like all crimes left unpunished, this would be something that happened again, and, after the second accuser, he was finally let go from the business. These events were shocking for the company but not the worst I have seen in a startup.

I would soon find out why some people can get away with murder in the business.

RED FLAG #2

After a couple more weeks in, word got around about my new role in the startup as I updated my LinkedIn page. A message from David popped up on my screen. The same guy that interviewed me four months ago and, according to Callum, lost his job due to under-performance. The message started, "I don't think you should be there. . ."

I asked if he'd be open to a brief phone call to which he said, "I don't think that's appropriate, but I hope you learn to protect yourself and don't do anything that will jeopardize your career." I read the message and shrugged.

Another friend request came in this time from a person named Kate. As I looked through her profile, something sent a chill down my spine. "V.P. of People—2018" it stated on her profile.

According to her timeline, she was the "infamous" HR Director that outlasted every other one of the predecessors but left as a disgruntled employee. I knew all these things due to the unprofessional manner in which they ran HR in this startup. It was an immature atmosphere.

If you ask any HR folks, they will tell you not to overshare stories about ex-employees. Especially the ones who walked away with a settlement. Kate was one of those employees, and the in-house counsel had just blabbered the tale to me on my first week.

I decided to reach out to her. "Hi, Kate, lovely to connect. I saw that you were previously here, too. I'd love to be able to pick your brain and learn from your experience if that's okay."

For a few weeks, there was no reply. But then I received a correspondence that consisted of very few lines. "If you need a new job, I'm happy to help out." That was it.

RED FLAG #3

From that moment on, I became cautious of what they expected of me in my role. I would often question and subtly challenge senior management decisions in hiring or promotions who had neither shown stellar records of high performance or relevant experience in their positions.

This startup was a company that didn't even have a performance management framework to start with, so how can they argue the ability of someone's performance? So, I started paying attention to "senior management" members. Who were they? How did they end up here?

Let's start with the Chief of Staff. The woman who greeted me on my first day. She didn't know any of the general needs and wants of running an HR team, but at first didn't seem unwilling to learn so. Naturally, I wondered how she earned this particular role when she, like most of the young hires here, had no experience in doing this type of job.

Usually, I am the first to champion and celebrate another female leader's success and to give her the recognition she deserves. But she was there to fill a "diversity" quota while the rest of the all-white millennial executives laughed behind her back. They treated her like a personal assistant. Still, as someone who obtained the position because of "who she knows," she had left herself with little to no credibility during my time there as I soon found out she had no intention to learn about anything HR related while managing this team.

Then we had the new joiner, "Talent Acquisition Manager," Tim. This individual brought a new recruiting team that was immediately earning higher salaries than all the other people on the team without any clear justification when one of the team members questioned.

This business was a company that represented itself as changemakers in salary transparency, so naturally this was not acceptable to the team.

I questioned this decision because, according to how they explained this ingenious concept of salary transparency, they meant it to be one step toward championing diversity. Yet, I've witnessed the intricacies of fidgeting the criterion to fool all their employees as to what is fair and what is not.

You see, every time a second role is hired, their salary must match the first regardless of how many years of experience and their previous earnings. In many ways, salary transparency should allow a company to hire the best talent for its needs. However, in this company, they would bump a roll up or down to allow for salary adjustments based on a few critical criteria.

Those granted a bump up were likely friends or family of a senior leader or men. They also disclosed to me that Tim was a longtime friend of Callum. So, you get the idea.

Let's look at Anna as another example. She was a vital part of the leadership team (non-executive), and her role was primarily to organize parties, lunches, and social gatherings for the company. While this type of position may seem like a redundant role in a corporate setting, it is a highly regarded position in startups due to its essential part to drive engagement with employees.

Startups call them "Engagement Leads." From the first time we collaborated together, Anna was hard working, willing to learn new things, tenacious, and resilient. These qualities are typical "go-getter" values and what we look for in a new hire. They are identified as A players in the startup world.

Anna's issue wasn't that she wasn't deserving of her role and the recognition she received, but there were underlying ways the company gave her a free pass in some sketchy ways. One of the first signs was when I was alerted of an undocumented bonus for Anna signed off by the CEO. I worked with her for four months, so you can imagine how disappointed I was to find out she was riding the nepotism wave, which was evident with her allowances for "lunch-tastings" or "venue scouting drinks" not allowed to anyone else.

THE AFTERMATH

I often ask myself, what did I learn from this? The truth about nepotism and how it infects our startups is right in front of me, every day. It starts with the founder and ends on their desk as well. Having inexperienced managers as CEOs can be disastrous to growth. A manager that only cares about the company, which might not seem like a bad thing, can be detrimental to your business.

It was evident to me that they only care about the revenue the company brings in and are willing to make unhealthy and unethical decisions to facilitate growth and "make it." People like this only care about themselves. When this happens, the culture can become toxic, with nepotism creeping in, ensuring that only the inner circle gets promoted.

Nepotism alone is terrible, but what can be more detrimental to a startup's culture is the fact that nepotism leads us to ill-informed, irrational decisions. The type of decisions that put inexperienced leaders in place that will, and have, taught them to accept unethical actions. Even things like fraud are acceptable by the company. Something like this happens to several startups when governance is non-existent, or there are no rules or policies to avoid these situations.

A startup will also suffer from a bevy of mediocre talent that the founders should have never hired in the first place. Unfortunately, most don't realize this until they look back in time. When folks invest in the company or who is on the board, they make recommendations to fill those hiring needs quickly, and most of the time, their suggestions are just not good enough.

The term "bros club" was an understatement of the unhealthy culture in this startup. To get ahead, one had to sleep with someone. This type of environment is hazardous, particularly for women. This eventually leads to the company becoming stagnant, and no new talent is willing to join the company as the word gets around.

Any prospective talent will see through the happy-go-lucky attitude projected on the surface and see the underlying toxic nature within the company.

COLLATERAL DAMAGE

The fact is investors have been encouraging this behavior for a very long time. This is because they don't care about "how" the company is built but "where" the company is going. This is quite short-sighted. Have we all learned nothing from the incidents that brought Uber down? I've spoken to an Uber executive who happened to be employed by Uber when it all went up in flames.

He said, "We knew it was happening. I wasn't physically there, but it was loud enough to spread through to the UK when I was in the role. We continued to ignore it, hoping for the best. A lot of talent from the early days departed, waiting for the penny to drop. None of us were surprised when it did, not like the outside world did. If the execs had some recognition or cared about the aftermath, we wouldn't be here today."—Operations Executive 2016, Kasper.[1]

What I've witnessed in the end was a company that had raised millions, hired family and friends with no real experience that contributed to low-quality output. Most of the time, they are railroading any real effort a team would have made towards a hiring or procurement process. I often think to myself, "If the new investors knew this was going on, they would probably not approve of this behavior." It wasn't as if it was a cheaper operating model.

Let's take a look at Payton. She was also an HR Director with a significant amount of respect in the business. She resigned without giving any notice. She just sent an email in the morning to the Chief of Staff about "not being able to do the job any longer." Then she shut her phone down to make sure she didn't have to discuss it any further. She didn't want to have any conversations about her departure, her team, or her manager. It was almost unheard of for a senior leader to resign in this way. It is considered cowardly.

"Honestly, I left because my mental health is so affected that I am ashamed to talk about what I've done in the last few months. I have put my career on hold for now," said Payton who was still distraught after she contacted me a week later.

---

[1]Kasper is a pen name for the interviewee who remains anonymous.

They deliberately put her in a position to resign because anything further with that company would have left her career scarred. The higher-ups instructed an HR practitioner to ignore her professionalism and do what was relatively best for the company. They set a fine line that they indicated she should cross, and it was all to serve the founder's purpose.

Unfortunately, a founder's mistakes aren't as apparent to the employees when you consider that the workforce is most likely inexperienced. They aren't able to discern if it was a wrong decision. That's why it is dangerous if a founder fails to get appropriate counsel full of experienced hands. The workforce ends up listening to their voice, which simply creates an echo chamber of what the founder says and emulating what the founder does.

The average age of an employee in our startup was 25 and 26, and their average tenure was six months. When I realized this, it solidified my standing as a misfit. Not only was I never going to be okay with the way things worked at this place. I was no longer interested in making it my destiny to change the culture for the better. I felt utterly outnumbered and worn out.

WHAT WAS NEXT?

Upon reflection, I realized this is a shared learning experience when it comes to startups. Would Callum have successfully maintained an elite, unfair, soul-crushing culture of the corporate world? The answer is probably no. His success resulted from not having actual rules and practices to govern his leadership, which would have been unlikely to achieve in a larger company—especially one bound by layers of democratic decisions.

When I left this company, I had learned to be careful when crossing paths with similar characters again. Especially one who had taken advantage of nepotism before realising it was terrible for everyone else around me. There wasn't much more I could do at that point but move on from a company like this. Whistleblowers might have assured that the company investigated a few issues. But, once the limelight has dimmed, they continue to get away with recklessly destroying their employees' mental health and careers because no one seems to be paying them any attention.

So, the next time my gut says yes despite all the red flags, I will make sure I say no.

My advice is this, avoid at the first instance if you can. If not, dig deep to find out what is really under that hood. To founders, you are the "in" thing at the moment, especially if you're Gen Z, but pay attention to the possible aftermath that will come down, even if you don't know it yet. So please, be respectful of your employees as your company will only be as good as your people.

Writing this has forced me to walk through these old experiences but with a new eye. In many ways, this was a terrible time for HR, and even worse, it was heartbreaking to be an HR leader. They forced me to work against my values every day, all to follow the rules and to appease what they call "the right HR for us."

They wanted me to execute actions that ignored the principles I hold dear to my heart without considering what that does to a person's mental health. They explicitly told my team to carry out tasks that, in some ways, felt to me like we were committing a crime.

As an HR professional, there is a constant fear of losing my job if I don't do as I am told. The more time I spent doing that job, the more I realized I wasn't the only one who felt this way. This fear lasted a few months until one day; I knew that the risk of damaging my reputation and ruining my career would be a far greater letdown than losing this one job.

If any founders are reading this, I hope you are taking notes. When you hire an HR professional, keep an ear open to what they have to say. No one gets to the top alone, and the first step is taking care of the people who work for you. When you do that, you will succeed. What's the best way to achieve employee happiness? Hire a fantastic HR professional and don't weigh them down with rules and policies. Listen to what they have to say. Employee relations is their area of expertize so let them thrive. By doing so, you will enhance productivity and be fruitful.

CHAPTER 2

The Type A

The experiences I'm sharing here are memories I sometimes wish I could erase. But there's no denying that they have shaped me into the person I am today. It's what I'm known for, both the good and the bad.

You may have seen headlines like the following;

Applet Becomes the Youngest Startup to Enter the Unicorn Club in 18 Months!

Or

Pics Becomes a Unicorn After a Rocky Slow Start

Or

UK Startup Becomes Renewal Energy Giant After Closing Funding with Top Tier VCs

When the media describes the success of a startup, they rarely discuss the sacrifice employees had to make to reach the point of victory. Why? Because that's not what sells newspapers. Plus, nobody wants to get into libel suits, especially when the limelight is already on them.

Many people have asked me what it was like working for such an exciting rising startup. Back in the day, I would reply like a broken record, "It is a great company! We're still young, but we're very ambitious, and the most important part, we hire super-smart people. We've had a lot of fun building this together."

If you have followed the recent hiring trends sufficiently, you've likely seen journalists discuss the lack of diversity in companies. This absence of diversification is especially evident in tech startups where the industry already suffers from a scarcity of suitable candidates.

A lack of diversity can unintentionally create unsafe and toxic working environments, which subsequently contribute regularly to high turnover. Founders push this disparity further when employees don't feel like they fit in mindfully. And they're unlikely to stay on in these companies.

But this isn't a story about employees not fitting in because they were different and unaccepted. This story is about a startup whose leader did not prioritize its duty to develop a good work culture. Instead, he spent all his time creating a fearful culture plagued by a performance-obsessed and uncontrollably dysfunctional workforce. His army of managers lacked both self-awareness and social empathy.

Whenever employees' productivity was affected, the well-being of the office continued to be disregarded to the point that it became not an option to be different. This startup was successful because the Founder only wanted to play with his kind, the Type A personality.

IT BEGINS

As I walked into what I thought to myself was my dream job, I looked at the 40 of us around the open-planned office that morning. I walked in and said, "Hi, I'm Sophie, and I'm here to build this rocket ship together with you. I cannot wait!"

I spoke with a trembling voice because this was a first-time experience for me. I was walking into a job with a startup and surrounded by peers my interviewer described as nothing but Class A people. I wasn't sure I'd properly fit in with my associates.

When you've spent most of your career in the corporate world, you forget that you're an individual with something to offer. You're not just a bum on the seat. Some of you reading this may disagree, or you may have had a more rewarding job. For me, at 27, I wanted this new job to take me out of that dead-end place I'd been wallowing in and hopefully change my perception forever.

And it did, but we'll get to that later.

When I began with this startup, the higher-ups repeatedly mentioned that this "will be one of those places that will only hire the best people. We're not in the business to wait for people to grow and develop into better versions of themselves. No. When working here, you should be fully qualified to do the job we hired you to do. So, make sure you do whatever it takes not to let anyone but 'us' in and do it fast. Once they're in, keep them."

I would soon find out that this monolog was not a joke. The interviewer meant "us" literally.

My first and only task was simple. They would measure my success, and when I passed, the rewards would be more than satisfactory. I was going to be responsible for putting in place these "rewards" that would chain our people to their jobs for a long, long time.

Sometimes in your life, you realize it's not worth it anymore. I know it may sound daunting, but when I was so high up in my newly created pleasing world, I was as addicted to this life as I would have been to morphine.

I did not just learn to do this on my own from day one. The Founder CEO would make sure the culture reflects what he believes is right. We, the employees, will faithfully follow, single file, until we morphed into these ambassadors of one of the most toxic workplaces I've ever known.

MONTH 1—FIRST RULE OF ORDER

It was about 7:00 p.m. at the end of my first day. I looked around the office and saw everyone still glued to their desks, eyes squinting tirelessly behind their glasses, noticeably worn out. I knew it was late and was sure that staring into those glaring 21-inch state-of-the-art extended monitors didn't help. All of the employees were typing, furiously trying to finish some last-minute work, so I assumed.

About three-quarters of the room was still full, so I thought there must be a tight deadline on a project. After all, this was my first day, and I had yet to know every inch of the company.

I turned to a new colleague standing next to me and asked, "Is there an urgent delivery or something? I can't believe most of the people are still here at this hour?"

My coworker's warm face turned toward the nearly full room and replied firmly, "I don't think anyone leaves this early. Why? Have you finished all your work already?"

I didn't understand his question at first. Was he implying that my work was less critical, therefore, there wasn't as much? Or did he mean that this was the norm, and it is what was expected? Or was it just me being a total alien in this new environment?

The custom of staying this late was difficult for me to understand. When working at IBM, I would have been halfway home on the tube ride, and at 6:00 p.m., our large cold concrete corporate office would have been a ghost town.

"Oh," I said, surprised. "I was just curious because it is kind of late now. Anyway, I'll see you tomorrow!" I dashed off quickly since I was late for dinner to celebrate my first day at my new job. When I started to leave, I saw a trail of people slowly pack up and stand from their seats. It was like they were waiting for someone to make the first move. "Strange," I thought.

As I made my way out, I set a mental reminder to speak to the leadership team about it tomorrow, primarily out of curiosity. I also wanted to warn them of the detrimental effects of a strained workforce.

Day two started while I was still taking off my jacket to get settled. Nik, the CEO, came up to me with a dry "Good morning, let's take a walk." I soon realized that this routine would become a regular thing. Whenever he said, "let's take a walk," it meant "let me tell you what you need to do next."

And so, I did. We took our first "walk."

"How did your first day go?" Nik asked. "Settled and ready?"

"Yeah, it was great. Everyone's friendly. They're all super smart, like you pointed out before. I can't wait to get sucked in!"

"Great, so here's the thing, some of us are hard workers, and there's a lot to accomplish in a short period. It's always going to be the kind of place where everything is urgent. So, I need you to set a good example."

"Oh," I said. "What do you mean?"

"If you leave early, they'll think it's okay, too. But that's just lazy behavior."

Based on the crispness of his voice and the way it trailed off after that last sentence, I knew this wasn't a joke. He meant that employees who don't stay well into the night don't work hard enough and are simply lazy employees.

"Well," I asked, sounding confused. "What if someone has personal circumstances or maybe, I don't know, has dinner plans or something?"

"Most of us don't have a personal life here. But that's life in a startup, whichever one you go to."

I was convinced because I was a total rookie.

From that day forward, I sold my soul to this startup. I embraced the norm projected onto me. And, while I was enduring the day-to-day, I figured there must be something I could do to make this just a tad more enjoyable for everyone.

First, they supplied free dinners to the employees without knowing there was a catch. Dinners are complimentary ONLY if you ordered from the business account AND after 8:00 p.m. And the meals had to be delivered to the office.

This practice certainly wasn't new. At the time, all startups supplied comfortable bean bags with foosball tables by default. Ours was an open plan office of dual monitors per desk. The reason for this was because it helps someone get their work done much faster.

Also, when we ordered dinner, employees were required to eat at their desks. There were a few people who would eat in a group, but most didn't. So, you get the gist. We were deliberately making sure our employees stayed locked in the seats with a ghost chain.

Then came the free breakfasts before 8:00 a.m. "Take your pick of coffee and croissant from the café upstairs. But don't forget to also take your laptop with you, by the way."

Sure, some of you must be thinking, "If giants like Google or LinkedIn get to be called Best Workplace of the Year by providing similar benefits, then it must be the right thing to do."

It definitely would have been right if we did not purposely orchestrate this to get more out of our employees. So, there you go.

By this time, I was still in my honeymoon period in the company. "This is the high life," I thought to myself, indeed. We all work hard with all this free food, and we don't even need to expense it.

I was used to the hard-knock life at IBM where a single £2.50 coffee receipt needed to be approved. Coffee, mind you, that I desperately needed to stay awake. They would scrutinize receipts even when they were the ones who sent me to Cardiff to a client meeting at 6:45 in the morning. They sent me at that time because that would have been the cheapest off-peak train ticket. Then the manager rejected that coffee receipt because it was deemed "non-essential."

So yes, this free food at the startup was the highflyer life I had been waiting for. I knew I had to ride this as long as I could endure. And it was only the first month.

MONTH 2—THE PRINCIPLES BECAME DEMANDS, A MEASURE OF YOUR PERFORMANCE

I was high on the Kool-Aid at this point, and we were quickly one of the best startups out there. Candidates were starting to flock to our LinkedIn Inboxes and website. They all wanted in. We had SO many options.

So, what was our first reaction? Tighten our hiring process to look for top-of-class A talent.

The cherry on top of the icing was no longer good enough. Nik made that clear.

Our extended hours became an expectation. We would ask them behavioral questions in the hiring process to ensure that we were only progressing candidates who had shown a pattern or track record of being "okay" working long hours. We used trick questions like "say there's a deadline tomorrow and you're about 30 percent done for your assignment. What would you do and why?"

We weren't looking for answers that told us they would work hard or work smart to complete it. We were specifically looking for people who would say "overnight," "whatever it takes," "however tired I would be." Because we wanted to make sure our potential employees were only high performers with no boundaries.

Today, I say this is wrong because I've been through enough therapy sessions to know. My doctor reminds me that I can have responsible relationships in my life only if I create boundaries myself. We were conscientiously taking that choice away from our employees.

Then, we would only hire these candidates if they fit into our personality mold. Before we had figured out what "type" of people we were and who we wanted, I had carried out a personality mapping of all the employees using the Enneagram method.

The findings were not all that shocking, but if this were not for a professional environment, I would have thought that we had an incredibly complimentary family. Our Leader was a Type 1, and the rest of us were Type 3s, Type 5s, or Type 8s, all of whom are perfectly believable followers of Type 1.

The Enneagram method is a type of personality test that you commonly find for free online. There have been various definitions to the types, but those that would classify as unhealthy Type 1s, happen to be uncompromising and pedantic visionaries. Type 3s have an over-expressed need for achievement and innate narcissism, Type 5s are intellectually arrogant and selfish, and finally, Type 8s are domineering and aggressive in a threatening world. All but the Type 1s share the same blind spot, vulnerability towards their leaders.

I couldn't tell if it was the culture we had all gotten so accustomed to and that transformed us into these personalities. Or were we innately like these types before we joined this startup? I was too blind to see the truth as I was categorically ecstatic to know I fit right in. I was a Type 8.

Moving forward, we would only hire these same types of candidates. Anyone who fell out of this group would not be chosen as we saw them as weak and too vulnerable to work with us. We took pride in creating an egocentric, narcissistic culture with low empathy but high-performing individuals.

"Is this right?" I would ask my colleague, Sylvia. "If we don't introduce some different personalities, don't you think we're always going to be a boy's club? I mean, look around us, we are two of three women in a group of 70?"

Sylvia, one of our managers and a close confidante of mine, said, "We are all so similar. That's why it works. It probably will not work anywhere else, but it does here because Nik has only ever allowed these types of characters to come close. Let's not disrupt it by adding a different mix in here. So, what if we're a boy's club? We're the lucky girls."

"But," I continued, "the constant need to compete and stab each other in the back, surely that makes you uncomfortable, too?"

"No," she said. "Not really. It's the same anywhere you go. This is just financial services for you."

"Do you feel included?" I asked her.

"Yes," she replied. "Of course. I'm part of almost every conversation because we're the same kind. And honestly, I find it invigorating because it just means people truly care about the work they put out there."

"I guess. . . ," I said, wanting to believe her.

"Maybe you're just not used to being surrounded by super dedicated people. Trust me. This is okay."

"Alright," I said. "I guess . . ."

If there was a day, I finally learned the meaning of "drinking the Kool-Aid," this conversation with Sylvia had taught it to me.

Shortly after I left the company, Sylvia moved on to something else, and as we reconnected, we also shared our therapy contacts.

MONTHS WENT BY

When we first started, we got the crowd's pick. Then we filtered through them to keep the very best. Now, our tolerance got thinner, and boundaries became non-existent. We turned arrogant, and we told ourselves it was okay.

Before I saw what was happening, I started firing more people than we were hiring. When I say "I," it's because the logic is quite simple. You see, it had become so much of a norm that these managers, who were hardly qualified, started growing intolerant towards the staff who were not performing by their standards.

Nik would put so much pressure on these managers to move at lightning speed that they would be the next on the firing line if they failed. No one was safe, but these managers were fully prepared to tackle it by buying time. As they willingly blamed their teams, Nik would be pleased to see that his prized deputies were not wasting time and were swiftly firing people. He called this "efficient leadership at its best."

Thinking about this earlier memory made me squirm with anguish.

Andy sent me a message on Slack at 6:00 a.m. that morning.

"Sophie, we need to fire these two people. They're not performing and have failed their targets."

"They have been here a month," I replied. "Are you sure they have FAILED?"

"Yes, they have. They're just not cutting it."

"What does that exactly mean?" I pushed, wanting to know more.

"They're just too slow for what I need."

"Okay," I answered. "Have you communicated any of this to them yet? What is your plan?"

"I'm going to send them a Slack message now that we no longer need them. I expect HR will sort out the paperwork?"

"Are you saying you won't even give them a call at all?" I asked, surprised.

"If there's no good reason, then I won't."

"Of course," I said

Then, off I went and did the deed. These calls were brutal.

Anyone that has told a person they have lost their jobs will tell you there is no joy in it. But, informing them on behalf of these managers was one of the worst messages I've ever had to pass on.

I know some of you reading this must be thinking that, of course, it should have been my job to do so. I was the only HR person, after all. But I also now know why you might think this way because you probably believe in the same things Andy did.

Andy is one of our up and rising stars of a manager. He had just graduated from university the previous year and since joining the company, had worked side by side, day and night, with Nik. Calling Andy, a reflection of Nik is an understatement. At this point, he would have already been using the exact words Nik uses, such as "slow," "not good enough," "stop wasting my time," and the famous "what are you doing here still?" Both Andy and Nik regularly directed these comments and questions to staff and colleagues who were then deemed to be "Not A players."

Before all of this exodus started, Nik once said to me over lunch, "Don't overcomplicate it. We were clear to them from the start. So, if they cannot perform, they must go. Also, per employment law, we don't have to give anyone any reasons to be terminated within the first two years, so just get it done."

He wasn't right, but he wasn't all wrong either. Sure, there is a loophole here somewhere, but it isn't the same as saying, "We are not a charity to keep them around." At our startup, these employees weren't viewed as a cost liability. Instead, Nik was adamant that there is simply no seat for people who are not "smart" enough to share this space. How can I be sure? Because employee cost was the least of our issues then.

This other time happened when I was in Poland, visiting the office we had just set up the previous month. So, by calculation, these were employees as fresh as one month old in tenure.

"Sophie, we need to fire the new head of department."

"Okay," I said. "What's the reason?"

"She's not fast enough. I think she might be too old for this job."

"Right," I replied.

"I suggest we keep the age entry young and fresh so that we don't risk delays."

"You can't say that," I warned.

One of the executives stepped in and explained to me, "Well, look, everything is replaceable. This chair I'm sitting on is replaceable, that table over there is replaceable, and you," and he pointed his coffee cup at me, "are also replaceable. Right?"

Yes, believe it. It happened, and they said that.

When I repeated this logic to my husband, he sternly said to me, "Do you even hear yourself?" I suppose I was still under the influence of the Kool-Aid.

About five of us reported directly to the founder. What this means is we were working in close proximity with him, and I found myself mimicking his behaviors. Monkey see monkey do, right?

I became an appalling and fearful manager, just like Andy. I would set clear but mostly unattainable success metrics for my team while openly indicating that they would have no jobs to come back to next month if they failed to hit those targets.

Why did I do this? Because I won't have a job to come back to if they fail me. By my logic, we have all failed Nik. This was what it was like every day. My colleagues and I felt like we were never good enough for this place. Even when we did feel good enough, it would only last for a moment because as you complete one task, the next one is just waiting behind.

My team would end up in a revolving door because there was no shame in being a manager who couldn't hold their teams together. By right, these were failures that we simply couldn't retain. Or more so, the toxic culture had chewed and spat them right back out.

They would praise me for being decisive, but my subconscious would be telling me my actions were nothing to be proud of. I learned to feel lost, or more so stuck, in the middle of the two, not knowing which way out was the better one.

GOODBYES

A goodbye is usually used on occasions where you would express good wishes when parting ways. The goodbye in this story is implied by a series of one-word conversations and a cold, soul-piercing revelation.

On one fateful day, I braved myself to free my soul from the God-forsaken toxicity. I know it sounds dramatic, but you have to be there to understand it.

My eyes were weary, not because I was feeling sad about bidding goodbye to the company. I spent the night crying after an all-night argument with my husband about how this so-called dedication turned into an obsession for my job. It was affecting my almost non-existent personal life.

"I think you need to quit...," Brooke's voice tracked with such sympathy as she watched my anxiety show in mere seconds.

"Yes, me too," I replied.

For the first time in ten months, I was sure of my decision.

This marked the point where I had already been struggling with sleepless nights due to increased anxiety. My panic would rise when-ever my phone rang, and I saw a message from Nik instructing me to do more damage to our workforce.

I had just returned from a recruitment campaign in New York. A last hurrah, so to speak, when I stood there in the room filled with hundreds of potential candidates. We were trying to convince them that working for us was a fantastic opportunity. I put on a straight face and allowed it to escape my mouth.

For three days, I told applicants that their lives would change after working for such an aggressive startup like ours because they would achieve more than they would in other places. Plus, we offered excellent benefits, including free travel, complimentary breakfast, free coffee, state-of-the-art laptops, and dual monitors. Don't forget our great free dinners, at the office, every night for as long as you are employed.

Hook. Bait. Reel.

We were on yet another flight to Berlin, this time for a client meeting, and Brooke looked at my pale face and asked, "What's wrong?"

"Nothing, just another message from Nik about something I need to do as soon as we land. And while I'm on leave. It's fine, really. . . ," I replied, trying to avoid her gaze.

"No, it is not. You haven't slept in 37 hours, and it's also 6:30 a.m. Whatever it is, it can wait. Today is your legit day off."

Brooke was firm this time about me taking the day to recover.

Of course, I didn't. We landed an hour and 20 minutes later to drop our bags off at the early check-in and then went straight to our temporary office. We did stop and got a nice coffee on the way in, so that was as far as I could remember about anything pleasant during that last trip.

As I got back into our London office the following evening, I asked Nik for a "walk." He looked up at me, nodded, and took his laptop with him while we paced towards the deserted shared kitchen area. We sat down, his eyes back on his computer, waiting for me to speak. I embraced my courage as I let the words escape from my mind. "I'm sorry, but this is it for me. I'm resigning."

I gave it a few seconds and then gasped with a sense of relief. I was prepared to carry on my speech but was interrupted with a cold. "Okay."

He slammed his laptop, stood up, and walked away. That was the last time we spoke.

I was left in a state of shock and liberation at the same time. I mindfully patted myself on the shoulder after I had done it. I had given myself a chance to be alive again without carrying the constant grief and guilt of doing the wrong thing by others. I was ready to finish my last pieces of work and call it a day. I started packing up my things and was carefully thinking about which bath bomb I would use tonight. I was also thinking about what I would like to pick up for dinner on the way home.

Peter, another close peer of mine, called as I made my way out of the building.

"Are you sure you don't want to reconsider this?" Peter asked. "You've come this far, and I know it's not easy, well most days were horrible, but we can all help each other get through it."

You see, the thing is, Peter, or any of my colleagues, couldn't help me even if they tried. Our roles were quite different. They were responsible for the other assets, and I was in charge of people. Our people. The same people to whom I presented fake propositions of great working culture.

The same people who, by direct orders from my manager, I was not allowed to address any mental health issues if brought up. These were the same people who would be left in utter shock when I told them their managers no longer needed them after 14 days because they were either too old or too slow for this. And the very same people who we denied all accounts of responsibility towards because it was, simply, never our fault.

"I don't think you get it, Pete," I replied. "It may not affect most of you, but this place has done its worst to me. I'm in control of creating these rules, guardrails, and processes that will continue to encourage these behaviors because it's my job, my task to complete. I cannot, with good conscience, continue to do this to myself and our employees. I wish I weren't in HR, but sadly, I am."

A week later, Brooke resigned. Then came Jake the week after. Inconveniently, I had started a trend and the subsequent departure trail.

THE AFTERMATH

The first few months of withdrawal were difficult; I had already moved on and found myself a haven compared to where I was. Yet, the fear of missing out was surreal. I would compare my incredibly supportive colleagues with the previously mendacious cohorts and miss them instead. I would watch the company continue to grow rapidly and feel bad for myself when I realized I was "one of the replaceable furniture."

But this is what we need to stop doing, especially if we find ourselves in a similar situation. The free dinners were put in place not to reward us for our hard work. They were implemented to entice us to work even harder and forget that we could have a life beyond those walls.

Yes, the shares scheme is a standard protocol to bind you for 12 months before releasing any of those "options." But you would have to sell your soul in exchange for them. Now, most of our alumni have moved on to better pastures for sure, but it doesn't mean they're not still battling with the trauma inflicted on them from the toxicity. We had an alumni support group believe it or not, and it was the most critical therapy in our lives for a mere moment.

Take Bianca[1] for instance, whom I reconnected with recently on how she reflected our joint past as she caught up on the new chapter of her life.

So, Bianca, you're a life coach now. Our readers want to know, did you learn anything from this experience that you felt has helped your clients so far?

"I believe that everything in life shapes us and people with us for a reason or a season, and I know this from my own startup experience. That was the case. I felt very inspired. Ironically, not at the time whilst at the company to become a life coach. I was mentoring and helping a lot of fellow colleagues there. By default, I didn't know I was actually mentoring and helping them; I just thought I was being mean.

---

[1]Bianca is an ex-employee and interviewee who remains anonymous.

And then I ended up becoming a life coach, and now I specifically help people with their careers and their relationships and to find deeper levels of honesty, so they can actually effectively communicate with one another. And this has helped my clients tenfold because I've been in environments where people don't communicate. And being in environments where people do now, the difference is astounding. Connection, openness, truth, and honesty are one hundred times better. . ."

Why do you think some entrepreneurs or founders create such a toxic environment?

"My opinion on why some entrepreneurs or founders can create such a toxic environment is because what they're creating is coming from a place of pain. Or a place of 'I'm going to show you,' or a place of ego like 'look at me, I can be successful, I can prove myself, and I can prove something.'

I can't speak for anyone's experience, and I can't say that that is how everyone operates from a startup environment. But the founders and the mental health of the founders and the founders' connection to empathy, compassion, what it means to be human is a major sector, and whether or not employees feel safe.

Whether or not employees feel like they can thrive, whether they can ask questions. And what I noticed is when there is hostility or a lack of care from founders, there's a real lack of communication. A lot of things get lost in translation. And people don't ask for help and support, and I believe what makes us human is being supportive and caring toward one another whilst having a common goal."

As someone who has experienced this type of toxic work climate, what do you think needs to be different to create an opposite environment?

"I think what needs to be different when it comes to startups is this balance of masculine and feminine energy, and what I've noticed in the startups that I've been in is there's a real sense of urgency to get things done. I believe that, yes, that is valid. At times we do need just to put our heads down.

So, get things done. But a lot of the time, when we're busy getting things done, we oversee the big picture and end up making ten million more mistakes. And from this place, we have to go back and try and rebuild a bridge that we've burned to smithereens. So, I think finding a balance between doing and observing and analyzing in communicating is more feminine energy.

So, I don't think that there needs to be the total opposite. I think there needs to be a balance between doing and being the masculine and feminine. The 'let's get shit done' versus 'Hey, let's just take a moment because we don't have the answers right now, and let's get some more clarity.'

Gavin on the other hand, is another ex-colleague who had remained a friend. In the winter of 2017, Andy summoned me yet again to give Gavin the bad news just after he had been our Country Manager for Western Europe. To my surprise, he jumped in instantly to give me his insights of the experience.

"As you've worked in different startups since, why do you think founders who have huge influences on how their employees work affect the culture so much?" I started off.

"I think it's so important. I mean, if the founder didn't affect the culture so much, it wouldn't have been so difficult to work in. But then, I also feel that the managers I had were such a shadow of the founder. Because it was a boy's club, right? So, if they want to be spotted for promotions, they need to do what the founder says. I think it's very obvious why Andy was enjoying it more than anyone else. Since then, I have realized that good companies have good founders. You can tell from a mile away. . ." As he let out a loud sigh finishing this sentence but clarified that he does indeed feel grateful to have been able to draw from these experiences now.

Some of them kept their trauma in silence and pushed it far into the back of their amygdala. You still see the evidence from the look on their faces. They cringe a little before they smile back at your question while they remember how it was.

The company has since gone on to be known for the best and the worst of its kind in the last four years as it stayed true to its first principle, "hire only the best people." Because of this, they were seen to suffer from diversity and inclusion. The boys' club remained thick and strong with bro-codes and macho nicknames for those still making "cutthroat" decisions.

The business also went through long months of the media dragging it through the mud with a bad employer reputation. There were multiple abusive and toxic culture allegations floating around. While the satire went out into the public arena, the company continued to power through it with ignorance. That was until their people got tired of talking about its shenanigans.

After all, our communications director used to say, "Any publicity is good publicity." So, there you go.

Fifteen people out of the 40 that started this journey with me that fateful year have all since resigned or left for some more unfortunate end. A long overdue catch-up earlier this year revealed that none of them would return even if life compelled them.

Their first question was, "Is he still there?" When they learned the answer was "yes," they answered with a "no."

I guess this just isn't the kind of company that has boomerang employees for obvious reasons. Would you return to a company with this type of environment?

And when the mass exodus started sometime in the Autumn of 2018, my inbox was filled with requests from journalists to speak out.

As I declined their requests politely, the journalist from Wired reminded me, "It's essential to me that the people that were there at the time feel vindicated by this. The hope is that it helps change the company and stops this kind of thing from happening elsewhere."

My contract didn't have a gag order, but I did not think my point of view was worth mentioning. Because there were already so many people affected by what we had created in the early days, they were impacted by the behaviors we encouraged as leaders when we could have prevented it.

I was overwhelmed with guilt. I was part of the rip-off, and I certainly was not proud or eager to let the world know.

Over the years, I would carry this badge of honor and proclaim, "It was an okay experience. It wasn't perfect, but no company is. I guess there is no difference from that place to any other fast-emerging startup suffering from growing pains."

PRESENT

So, you must be thinking, why tell my story now?

Because nobody deserves this and I hope you can learn from my mistakes one way or another.

Half a decade later, people still ask for my personal opinion and apply for a job there. They come to me when they're unsure if the whole toxic culture was real or just media hype.

My answer is blunt, "There are enough articles out there to help you make your decision, no?"

Just last week, another HR consultant was on a consulting call with a FinTech we were both going to pitch to and the first thing she said was, "We have both built and scaled startups. But we would never do what Revolut has done to its culture. So, rest assured we know what we're doing."

The client followed up with a vast and obvious sense of relief. Wherever I go now, I'm either proud of what I survived or mortified to be recognized for "that HR lady in that toxic place."

Learning from a founder like Nik isn't considered a consolation. In any case, this was most definitely a jackpot to me. I had my first big break in startups, swimming upstream, learning what red flags to look out for and how some personalities are too naïve to change. For some people, the narcissist in them lives on.

I became more alert when looking for new roles or met other startup founders trying to avoid similar characteristics. Luckily, as I swam past this sea of distress and regret, I also began to recognize the privilege when meeting founders who want to treat their people well. They do so without being asked or told.

I'm glad this experience hasn't stopped me from believing there is good in some employers. I just wasn't lucky enough the first time around, and I hope this never happens to you.

CHAPTER 3

The Talent Acquirer

Every time I read the startup news, I find a unicorn popping up or another startup that has outgrown itself in the shortest period. We all become so excited about these new businesses when we read titles like,

N26 reaches 1000 employees in 6 months.

Elemy reaches unicorn status, at 1000 people in 17 months.

New unicorn startup Hopin triples its employees in mere 8 months!

What does this tell you? It tells me that these companies have gone through tremendous growth and are labeled as massive successes to their investors and the public. There is a constant stream of demand for their products. And their capital is secured by growing the teams building these solutions.

There is absolutely no shame in this. However, I find these articles to be incredibly misleading. What we fail to notice is that these companies get a head start with this good publicity. They talk about how much they've grown. Then, we see headlines like "Uber's culture takes a hit as we witness mass exodus this summer."

Every time I read a piece of news like this; it makes me cringe a little. My skin crawls because I have lived through it. I've experienced this from the inside many times. It feels like this type of evolution is doomed to repeat itself again and again. My usual reflex is to do a little bit more digging. I do this by asking the following questions.

How many employees left before they hit the first 1000?
How long did it take them to get to the first 1000?
How big is their team?
How long has their people team been there?
Do they just do recruitment?
What do their Glassdoor reviews say?

I'm flagging this trend because these are the things that should keep us awake. Especially if we're working for those companies, these are the questions we should be asking ourselves or the company when interviewing with them. Remember, "Rome wasn't built in a day!"

I took the liberty of interviewing their senior recruiter, Martin[1] at Hopin.

How fast are you growing at Hopin? What are the numbers like?

"So, we are almost 1000 people now, and we were maybe 20 or 50 in 2019—(We were) doubling headcount within...four months that's the speed of the number of people that came in. To put it into context, at my last company, we had 10 in (the) recruitment team overall, and the startup went from 50 to 300 in 12 months. I'm now in a team of 40 recruiters."

Obviously, being internal, you've seen how the targets are being set. What would you say are some of the main reasons recruitment is just driven nonstop?

"To be honest, the headcount is very arbitrary. I always ask whether this is even good or bad hiring or why are we hiring this many people in this period of time? From my experience, you never have concrete hiring plans as much as this at that early stage. It's always been that we have to hire a lot of people because we're scaling, and we're growing at whatever scale, and we just have to do it. Usually, you don't have the sort of strategy that is very well defined for hiring at this stage. I've seen the pattern.

But as a recruiter, I don't think you'd get that context on a wider scale either. I think it's because it is difficult for them to agree on priorities on what we actually need. And I think it's dependent on the leaders whether one will shout louder and get

---

[1]Martin remains anonymous as a current employee of Hopin.

10 headcounts. Or another one will be considered less of an impact to the business if they get less headcounts.

I was in places where we could see these conversations around prioritization hiring plans and watch that not only was it very difficult to agree, but it is also very difficult to make final plans because, in startups, everything changes, right? And we operate in constant change. But how much of this is healthy, and how much of this is not? From my point of view, as a receiver and recruiter that then gets 20 positions to work on, I tell myself I shouldn't be even analyzing who came up with these decisions. I just needed to deliver.

So sometimes it is hard. Personally, I'm a person who would love to understand. I love a plan. I love a good strategy. But that feels like early on in a startup, it's just not really there and it is acceptable too."

In a couple of words, how would you describe Hopin's current culture?

"I would say transparent is (a new) kind of buzzword, but we actually do a lot here. We share a lot of information. We share the health of the business, how we're doing in terms of what our customers think, and what our customers' customers, or audiences, think about us and the product. There is a lot of transparency. Every week, you're going to know what's exactly in terms of the business's health.

What I learnt however is that what happened was abnormal for any business. Because Hopin went from a tiny little startup to a product and market fit from heaven. Customers coming to you asking how can you help us with your products, then VCs wake up and want to invest in the COVID kind of tools because the world is changing. It just served the entire planet overnight.

Because the way we live and communicate had suddenly changed, our expectations of who joins the company also slightly differed from what you would hire traditionally into a tech company. Some of the more curious people that I think we attract can adapt easier and also bring in a new way of working together. Linking it to our mission, I'd say we are huge on the emphasis of good communication and shared experiences.

The most distinctive one in our culture I would say is the purpose that initially was there when our CEO started the company, removing barriers to add accessibility to all. We set out to democratize access to everyone when we were all stuck at home. We have the kind of culture aligned around a purpose that is very tangible, easy to understand, and genuine. To me, that's key. Take my past experience for example, I've met a gambling marketing agency company with a purpose to help our users make smarter choices online. It was so blown-out-of-proportion however compared to what we were actually doing. It always felt like there was a disconnect when you're trying to apply this kind of aspirational purpose and mission to something that isn't quite fitting the optics it is showing. At Hopin, it's simple. It's what we all want."

WHAT IS PERFECT?

When I ask candidates what the "perfect" opportunity looks like for them, I usually get the same response: "I want to work at a growing startup that's doing something disruptive and could be the NEXT BIG THING."

Another problem that disturbs me is that these stories sell because it announces their enormous numbers, those significant milestones. Instead, we conveniently ignore the journey it took to get there. The teams responsible for successfully delivering these aggressive recruitment targets and the constantly tedious onboarding had to be carried out to ensure people knew on day one how to turn on their laptops.

By now, you must be wondering how this connects to the founder. Everything at this particular stage and everything the teams are doing comes from the founder's demand.

He just walked out of the investors' retreat, telling them that the company will be able to deliver this Rocket at a staggering shorter amount of time than its competitor coupled with a heavily discounted price just to acquire its first million customers. So yes, all of this comes back to who the founder is and what headspace they were in at the time.

The team, on the other hand, is also in an unfavorable state because of this.

If you've known or spoken to any HR people working in these teams in this type of demanding illogical environment, you know they absolutely loathe the experience. They usually come out the other end battered, embarrassed, and more importantly, ultimately defeated. Just try to imagine this weary team going against all they have learned to satisfy the company's demands because, frankly, their rent that month depended on it. I can tell you that it was not what they signed up for when they said yes to the job.

Let me show you the logic (estimated under ideal situations).

1. First, the head of the department joins and takes a minimum of two weeks to get settled.
2. They start hiring the HR team in Week 1.
3. Recruiters are functional in Week 4.
4. HR begins due diligence to find out what the employees need in Week 5.
5. Onboarding program takes priority in Week 6.

From Week 10 onward:

6. Manic begins as recruitment numbers overhaul the capacity of the current team.
7. HR starts panicking if every 100th person in a new country has been hired compliantly.

8. HR starts building development plans for employees under demands; however, the company has yet to determine its objectives.

9. Managers go into duress as performance reviews are up and they are expected to run without much preparation.

10. Recruitment targets increase and continue to take priority over everything else in this team.

11. Steps 6 through 10 go on repeat until the team burns out.

So, unless we're pretending that every step has a turnaround time of a mere one week, we can get all of this done in three months instead of six. Sure, then HR would be one of the most churned teams by choice in all companies. And the HR team is always the one who stuck around even after disasters hit them repeatedly. I am being skeptical here, but you get the gist.

Sadly, I have also been in that exact scenario multiple times. Yet, I still didn't learn what was wrong until I got a glimpse of what good looks like. Thousands of people my team hired thoroughly enjoyed their non-rushed weeklong onboarding. And we were able to be fully functional for longer than their probation period because of the care and attention we gave them. This longevity was thanks to training, development programs, and just good old effective managers. Imagine my disbelief that this could be achieved in a similar-sized startup.

When I met **Patricia Santos**, an HR leader and consultant for tech startups in Los Angeles, we discussed her experience in balancing the hypergrowth needs with sustaining a healthy culture. As she attributed the success to having a "human" founder, she talked to me about one of the best companies she had worked for, **Ring**. This US-based tech startup employed her until 2019. Amazon later acquired Ring.

What was the headcount when you left Ring after they were acquired?

"Over 2,000 in four years. We grew really fast, and Ring was just about 2,200 at that time. It (was) fun because Ring's culture was

strong before we even hit massive growth spurts, and it was very centered around the mission. We were based in Santa Monica and surrounded by these super thriving startups, but we weren't like any other startups around us. We didn't have the ping pong tables or the team-building events. We didn't do a lot of celebrations. It was like we were there to keep our neighborhood safe and that was enough for the people. It's the culture that drew out the kind of people who were most proud to say, wow, we work at Ring for this intangible purpose we so strongly believe in, and so we don't need all of the other things."

It also sounded like there was a great culture. Did Jamie influence much of how it turned out to be a great company to work for?

"We were there because we supported the mission and believed in Jamie. Jamie really showed (us) how good of a leader he was. Jamie was a caring person. And I wasn't the first person to be like, let's not celebrate anything like a Christmas event. I think (that was) the fun part about my time there. Even when it was painful, or (when we were) working as hard as we did because we were still working toward a mission.

So, any growing pains (we had), we got it together, and it never felt like a difference in moments. I never felt like it was us versus management or executives. We were all kind of like that, even (during) the acquisition with Amazon. That meant the culture; it was all Jamie, the founder. (He) cared about it, and it made such a difference compared to what we both had gone through in other companies.

This was his style. He's very hands-on—every new hire (became) a part of that culture. When there was anything we were unsure of, like during the acquisition, which was super stressful, people would go to him for ease. Or when people were feeling unsure about what was going on, they would turn to Jamie and ask, 'What do you think?'

He was so strong and reminded us we were there for the neighbors, and that was our mission, regardless of its acquisition. It was really fun. Yes, you grind but everyone around you believed in it."

Did you think that would have been doable if your team, say, was half the size? Or the time was much shorter?

"Every startup is going to be stressful. Especially the first few years but very quickly, we got bought out by Amazon. Even when we started thinking about going public really fast because of the conversations that Amazon started at such an early stage for us, I think that without Jamie's presence or his leadership style it would have been harder, which is true for all startups, especially in the early days.

His presence was just so (needed). He really tried to be in front of people, and he has a big personality. He was so present, even with our lives like remote teams carrying on past 3,000 people, past acquisition. We grew really fast, but we didn't become all 'fluffy' because we were in Santa Monica with other typical startup personalities.

A bunch of 'regular' startups were the other way where they're just growing so fast and have really smart people where toxicity or the density of moving fast were really unsustainable. If it wasn't for Jamie's leadership and influence, we probably wouldn't have been as successful. It was definitely uneasy when we first merged into Amazon. He protected our culture so that we didn't need to be like corporate, and he ensured we knew what he thought, and he really kind of reassured us that they bought the product to further our mission. Nothing more."

Why is this important to the company?

"I mean, we've got a great CEO going to work with. But if the CEO cares about all the people, except for the HR team, it won't work. Jamie was very involved in that way. So, he cared about it, but I think we were like the headcount piece, right? It's about prioritizing the right things. I think that the headcount just doesn't seem as important as getting that engineer to be sure the product ships and getting the head of marketing to know what we're doing on Facebook. I don't think I could have worked as well if Jamie hadn't been as invested in people as in HR. I think we always feel, especially in startups, that we do like small HR teams growing, grinding through it, and maybe it would have been a little more painful but doable. I don't know if the environment was, say the opposite, it would have worked as fast (and) as nicely as it did."

These are incredibly successful stories, but they are also very rare in the startup world. The success patterns show a reflection of the typology of its founder.

The type is too obsessed with just hiring to "look good" because the higher profile hires they make, the better they look to their competitors. The issue here is that the company's life depended on acquiring the talent until they took it too far. It's an example of a company using its newly acquired talent to win businesses. Otherwise, it won't be scalable.

Their time is mainly spent wooing new, high-profile talent instead of building a company of choice. They are often caught up debating the analogy of chicken and egg. Which comes first? Without the talent, you don't win clients. Without clients, why is the talent there?

And what if they genuinely don't care about people at all?

Marisa Bryan, a senior Talent Acquisition leader in multiple leading organizations globally, confirmed this assumption based on her revolting experiences in **Revolut** and a European Credit FinTech (**Company K**), both high-profiled unicorns in the European market.

I had an opportunity to sit down with Marisa and ask her some questions.

You must have seen a lot of hyper growth companies that are only focused on hiring. Why do you think they don't pay enough attention at the start about retention of their people?

"If we look at the psychology of human beings, we are naturally predisposed to instant gratification, right? Like the experiment on young children, you can have your sweets now, or you don't have them now. You can get them later instead. The child always chooses now. Same thing, but on a much bigger scale. You can have your people now versus big sorts of future problems. Which do you invest in? So is the current pain point versus a long-term view of where you need to get to."

And what if you're on the other side of the coin, as a candidate? How does the experience differ internally? (This is what Marisa had to say about her time at Company K.)

"During this time, I lead a team responsible for hiring their engineers. And this shouldn't come as a surprise to anyone, as they have a widely documented and available Glassdoor showing you their process of doing these logic tests for all employees regardless of their role and level. And (these tests) are essentially psychometric tests, a way to fit the missing tile into the pattern. And if you fail the test, it doesn't matter if you're a Ph.D. student from MIT; you don't get a job at this company.

And the reason the tests are in place is because the CEO (and) founder, has a personal belief that these logic tests act as an identifying factor of great talent.

(He) believed in (these tests) despite the team having presented volumes of data about candidates who had the right skills and experience but failed the logic tests for whatever reason. Or the surmountable candidates withdrawing because they were unwilling to submit themselves to the logic tests.

Countless debates and discussions on repeat, there was just absolutely no movement on removing them. And for me, you may be the most amazing company and have taken the world by storm. That's all good, but realistically part of being a great founder is listening. Being able to take onboard input and feedback from the people around you because it doesn't matter if you're Steve Jobs or Bill Gates, you don't know everything about everything. You know everything about Credit, and you've created this amazing product in Sweden, but I just think the kind of arrogance that I have experienced with this type of founder, believing, and feeling as though they know all aspects of running a company you are just not okay."

And as she crossed paths with **Revolut**.

"I went for a Global VP of Talent Acquisition role with them, and I was interviewed but immediately withdrew from the process while realizing a significant drawback from their process. It wasn't that I was being interviewed by an intern, but that there was no effort made whatsoever to get to know me as a person or to get to know my motivations. Like what am I passionate about? Why do I do the job that I do?

In the later stage, it got worse. It was just a series of questions about metrics. How many people do I need to recruit x amount of more people and still just zero interest in me as a person or my fit? To me, it is clear that's a reflection of what the Founder cares about, not you as a person or anyone else for that matter. Maybe he just cares what your outputs are, what you can deliver. And I know at least three people in my immediate network who have worked there and left within 12 months, all very senior, very experienced people. It shows until today there are the same few people who'd been there since day one.

But the biggest problem in this scenario is that we have used up all the time in the early stage, the most prominent stage to shape

*your culture, your brand and set up all the right foundations. (It)
was all wasted because we've ended up creating an environment
that isn't sustainable for scaling after. You start wondering what
went wrong in the first place."*

Your final piece of advice?

*"If done slowly and with respect, you can win. The business is
about people."*

BrewDog was an award-winning UK startup that crafts beer
before its employees called it out for creating a toxic working culture.
It was a company that grew too fast, sacrificing all the important things
they were meant to be building. Because of this, the company had no
foundation to fall back on when things started to break, and then disgruntled people left the company.

But let's not forget another important point: the size of the people's
team controls the focus of the team, affecting the final output of what
their employees will get right. It's basic logic. I am making this point
out loud because I've come across far too many startups hiring for their
first people manager in the middle of growth. They're even proud of it.

And I've been brought into these startups to "fix" this problem
that they first created themselves because it was so underwhelming or
unnecessary before. Some startups got it worse when they decided to
only bring people in under the "advice" of their investors.

RISE, COMPANY ONE

In the summer of 2020, I met the Founder/CEO of a startup in its second operating year. This was a fast-growing company at the time, with
already close to 200 people. They also had some big names on their
board and leadership team.

So, I was under the impression that they knew what they were
doing because they hired such fantastic talents. They had an incredibly

focused, ambitious founder, and we shared a lot in common. Naturally, the introduction-turned-request to help her "improve" her People Function was an invitation I didn't want to decline.

Also, after a few weeks of sharing what we both thought was "good" in startup culture, I set my expectations high in terms of what I'd expect in this company. As I came into the company, I was introduced to the current HR manager. I was immediately met with an overworked, burnt-out HR person who was already on the verge of resigning.

The COO managing this overwhelmed team of two also clarified from our introductions that she did not know how to handle this, nor did she have any experience developing a good People Function. Before the current HR manager, this small team had already churned another pair of HR and recruiting experts. When I dug a little deeper, it was clear that they paid too much attention to this team for their day-to-day. It was a classic case of an undervalued function of the business. Compared to how my discussions with the Founder started, you can only imagine my dismay.

"How did this happen?" became my opening line to every single meeting I had from that point onward.

"Where do we store the employee documents and profiles?"

"How do you know when your employees are happy or not?"

"Do you know what your culture is like?"

"Do we have a process for X,Y,Z?"

All of my questions were met with silence. In the meantime, recruitment was an ongoing campaign as they continued to hire close to 30 people every week, yet everything they needed, at the latest, should have been there a year ago.

We were at the point of 200 people with no development plans. We were in the middle of hiring another 50 without any succession planning or an optimized org chart design. This was the state of things. When I asked about the size of the people team, they told me it wasn't the focus. They felt it was more important to hire all these talents because they're the ones who win businesses and hit sales targets. So, there you go, I just walked right into another position as a "blind talent hunter."

Their Sales director was about to walk out.

Then came the resignation of the head of customer support.

To start, it took a team of three and me to bring all of the needed work together. We had to get them to a steady state because this created another problem I did not expect.

Once HR was formally introduced in the company to help "improve things," these unattended and uncared-for employees saw it as a desperate fix more than anything else. Overnight, after my introduction to the company, I got stacks of emails from employees, first welcoming me warmly and then ending their email with cries for help. Suddenly, our wheels were spinning. I saw flight risks (employees who were showing signs of resignations) at every corner.

Things started to calm down three months later, and we achieved it all amid that epic hiring campaign. There was onboarding, a system to record things, a database for employee files on a fully functional HRIS (human resource information system), and people were finally told of their career pathways and had development plans to reach their ambitions. It was a good day when we were able to let out a sigh of relief.

I'm not saying this has to be done by a people team. But at least by someone who knows what they're doing, not winging it by chance day by day. If it is the finance director who is doing this, so be it. But make good and right decisions to build the foundation for the company, please. If you don't know, ask for help as Sandra did.

She didn't do this on purpose, and in the end, it all worked out.

CRITEO, COMPANY TWO

Criteo was a very successful, publicly listed online advertising firm based in France. Before it hit the stock market, the Founder/CEO was quickly replaced by a much more experienced CEO. It started off as a company that scaled too quickly because the CEO only cared about what he thought was right. After a few years, the board decided that he wasn't the right person to lead the company, initially for reasons we weren't aware of. When I finally caught up to the truth a year later from an ex-employee, this was how Marianne,[2] their Head of HR described it.

"When it happened, it was just because he pushed his demands too far. First, he wanted to over hire because it meant we were bigger than another French Tech Unicorn. There was no good reason for it. Then, the CEO wanted to have an office in Palo Alto, although we didn't need it. He almost forced it. The leadership team, everyone, told him we couldn't compete in Palo Alto. He must have understood this but chose to ignore that because not only was our attrition insane, the salaries were off the charts. We went out of our way to transfer people from Paris to Palo Alto. But they were sometimes getting three or four times the salary to do precisely the same job. The salary increase was so that they could afford to live in Palo Alto. Because of that, the company lost a lot of money and the board wasn't happy."

"The team presented a load of data to show that we weren't producing anything in that office. But it was a real ego thing to have a presence in Palo Alto. And he wanted to be able to say, 'I built the first French Tech unicorn—unicorn. And look, we've got this office in Palo Alto.'"

"Then the auditors came in. They recommended that the first thing was to shut Palo Alto because of the amount of money it was costing them. Contrary to some typical patterns of failure, this was simple. It was because the right decisions were completely overruled with no justification other than 'Well, I'm the founder; therefore, what I say goes.'"

"Even the best leaders in the world listen to the people around them, and in a company, they have their board of directors, their trusted advisors around to guide them. I think we got lucky along the way, otherwise I don't think you'd see us today."

---

[2]Marianne is an ex-employee of Criteo who remains anonymous.

FIN, COMPANY THREE

Let's now talk about a startup who was so obsessed with hiring fantastic talent that they too forgot to look after their people somewhere along the journey. Except this time around, I was the one making this mistake.

Usually, when I'm the head of the people department, I am asked to look after two things: hiring the talent and looking after the talent. What happened here was that because we were still very small, my job only entailed the first part. So, hiring it was. Except this became my only job, for two whole years.

During my interview with the founders, I couldn't believe how lucky I was.

When we first met, Robert, the CEO said, "Forget what did not happen in your last company. From now on, you learn from your mistakes and bring your best version here. We're going to grow this company together."

Reliving this part of my memories always makes me smile. It was one of the better parts of my career so far.

So, we were only five people at that time, and I was tasked to hire our first 10, then 20, 30 people until we hit that sweet spot of 100 after 12 months. I spent my time with the team making us recognizable in all facets of FinTech. We had the podcasts, and we had the high-profile leadership team.

We had a bit of everything, and our candidates would jump on board to join us after the first interview. Even when company swag wasn't a default in your welcome pack yet, we had boxes of swag made every other week. Simply put, we were an attractive company.

And quite frankly, until this, I'd never done such easy recruitment. Of course, we enjoyed building this company together so much that we lost sight of what else was necessary, the sheer happiness of our employees.

With success after success, hiring became easy for us. We were almost addicted to the exhilaration of closing an offer and having the candidate say "Yes, I'll join you" with such excitement in their voice.

We were on a high to close more candidates, we wanted the power players in the industry, and we wanted them all around the globe. This was also partly driven by the fact that our clients were everywhere from London to Rwanda.

This was when remote working or a hybrid model wasn't an expected thing yet in startups. If you joined a company based in London, you're expected to show up in their London office and possibly entertain several overseas business trips. Of course, you could work from home, but your home would have to be in the same country at the very least.

What we had then set up was something called satellite offices. As the phrase explains, it was an office to "house" our employees based in remote places far away from the headquarters. In HR terms, this meant that it was a shell with nothing but tools for you to do your job and definitely not tools for you to succeed in the long term.

Why was this important?

Because being able to "employ" people compliantly was far more critical than retaining them; it was basic logic for us. If we can hire from all around the world, we are giving them the opportunity of their lives. This was the problem; we thought that we were more important than their careers. Also, the tragic part is that most employees don't realize this until they've been with a company long enough to ask for their next promotion. Like everyone else, they have joined this company based on its shiny offer 12 months ago.

Let's circle back. Where did we go wrong?

We lacked focus on supporting our people. While support comes in all shapes and forms, what employees ultimately want is to grow their careers in the company by having opportunities for advancements, learning platforms to help them hone their current skills, and improve on them until they eventually reach their goals.

One of the main driving forces behind this concept is that millennials also form the largest majority of the startup workforce. Therefore, these are employees who have been subjected to development programs from their early school days. They will always crave more space to sprout their needs in their companies naturally. They joined to throttle their careers because a corporate life won't give them that, so let's not forget this.

What do they *want* instead of what do we want to *give* them? Is it a paradox? Employers give them laptops because we want them to be mobile, but we don't ask if they work better with an extended monitor to sit on their permanent home desk. We kept at this for a long time, beyond the time we hit 200. This was also the point when we realized something was breaking. Something was falling apart. The company lost focus, and I lost focus.

First came the disgruntled complaints about no career progression, then came the low-performing team out of nowhere. Finally, the resignations arrived. We started losing people. These people were so passionate about our dreams together and decided they wanted to dream somewhere else. The same people we depended on for opening up new markets and opportunities with us because they dared to dream. We valued them, we praised them, we gifted them, but we didn't treasure them.

As puzzled as we were, we didn't stop to think about what we could have done to fix the problem. Instead, we quickly moved on from it, focusing on how to replace these leavers, which meant more recruitment coming up. This went on for another few months before we finally paused to re-evaluate where we went wrong.

Coupled with a few more resignations, this time from our newly hired junior employees, we began to worry. We were losing both our top and bottom, and to be honest, we were already lean to start with.

David announced in a meeting with me, "It's becoming apparent that we need to do more for our people because they are our biggest asset. I think we have lost sight of who we are and why we were winning in the beginning." He brought us back to our earlier journey. "No more distractions. They come first," he concluded.

The leadership team huddled together. This was when I, too, recovered my passion—creating an environment for employees to succeed and thrive, not merely survive. Just like any famous life lesson you learn, we picked ourselves up to Reset and Iterate. It was a fruitful time in our startup where we felt we were closer to our employees, and we knew what we needed to do, albeit still being 18 months old.

From learning what our people needed through engagement surveys and focus groups, we launched a series of changes that turned us into one of the top companies to work for that year alone. Yes, it was legit announced by LinkedIn, and there was also a celebratory party.

Employees would say, "Thanks for listening to us. I thought the focus groups were really helpful. A few weeks ago, I didn't think you would ever be able to change my mind about leaving."

"Don't thank me," I replied. "I'm sorry we didn't see this sooner. Thank you for holding on to the faith you had in us."

Since then, Bianca, just like our other employees, new and old, became an integral part of our performance review designs, just to name a few. We recognized that to give people what they want, we must include them. And then we tore down the ivory tower.

I'll be honest; however, it was a lucky turnaround for us because not all companies can turn a large ship around without causing more casualties.

CHAPTER 4

The Middle Manager

THE NEWS

A message came through. "Can you talk?," Yasmin asked.

It was 6:00 p.m. on a Friday, and we'd all had a pretty heavy week with disciplinaries—the standard people issues you normally find in a startup. Without overthinking it, I said "Yes, ring me." I could hear that she was probably at the park taking her evening walk.

"Hey, I am so sorry to do this to you, but I am resigning." I could almost picture her smiling. I knew straight away this was good news for her and she wanted it to be for me, too. It took me 15 minutes to feel a sense of relief, but then I was ecstatic for her as she talked me through her thought process and how this was an opportunity that she couldn't let pass.

"It was hard for me to break the news to you, but I knew that you would understand it because in a lot of ways, we are very similar. For the past two years, we have talked about my growth and I now feel I am now ready to be on my own. Push myself out of the box as you did many years ago... ," she trailed off.

"I understand, and I couldn't be more proud of you," I told her. "Everything we have worked on together was meant to lead to this day. And I am so happy to see you become this strong, confident version of yourself that will carry on to great things in life. Your career is just at the beginning. This is truly bittersweet for both of us."

She thanked me for all I had taught her over the two years she'd worked with me. Never once had we let each other down. We spent the next five minutes powering through what our next actions would be. Write a job advertisement for her role and post it on Monday and get a replacement as soon as we can. We drew up a whole game plan, and she sent through her confirmation of notice in the next hour.

As emotional as that conversation was, we were also pragmatic. This was our jam. We take on issues and quickly find solutions. This was the reason Yasmin was one of the best executives I had ever had the pleasure to work with, let alone coach. She was the kind of team player who would always come through regardless of how challenging a situation was and was never so short-sighted as to make careless decisions just to get by—which is common behavior in HR teams, especially in startups. Yet, that was never us. We'd created teams together and left companies together. This was the first time she'd left me behind. Yes, I say left behind because truly, she was moving on to take on a challenge bigger than what I was facing at that moment.

At first, I was shocked. I kept replaying it in my head during and after the phone call, "What could I have done differently to retain her?" And, of course, initially I felt a slight sense of betrayal after I hung up, but as I zoomed out, I mostly felt immense loss.

This was a huge loss for me. If our company had been ready at that time, she would have been promoted, had her own team to grow out, been able to polish her managerial skills, and we would have probably carried on working with each other for a lot longer. But it wasn't the right time, and I wasn't able to carve out a role rewarding enough for her in the organisation. It was the right time for her to go.

This is very personal for me to talk about because I have always held the reputation of being a rational leader—I am pragmatic and I make black-and-white decisions for the companies I represent. I would go on and carry out redundancies rationally and often be put in positions to get a company out of trouble. I was that person who would defend our company in tribunals and I never conceded unless there was a far better reason than reputational damage. But what I have learnt through this experience was that Yasmin wasn't actually the first to leave even when they worked in a supportive, empowering team. A few years back, Agnes, another smart and resilient young woman who was responsible for setting up and shaping the culture of my People team in Poland, left my team for the same reason.

PROVING THE SUSPICION

What I did next was to begin searching for the underlying cause of these "good leavers" in an organisation. I had to find a way to minimize this emotional loss for me and others who had been just as helpless as I was.

In reality, we were definitely not a startup without its own demons; misalignment of leadership, lack of development conversations with managers, poorly performing first time managers, and unaligned market compensations. But what we did was keep trying.

I started tracking (or backtracking I suppose) the "other" reasons behind leavers in our company. In any HR/People team you have met, HR professionals are told that it is crucial to investigate the reasons for leaving using these common categories; Culture, Managers, Personal, and Under Performance. Now let's take a closer look at Culture and Personal in particular. We describe "Culture" as "How aligned are employees with the values and working principles of the company" and "Personal" as "Any other reasons that are not truly revealed as the employee worries for the effect it will have on their future references."

It might as well just be called "The real reasons we can't seem to figure it out." So, I spent 12 months reconnecting with "leavers" from the past (I took a sample test over a four-year period) and drew a conclusion that more than 88 percent of these "Personal Reasons" leavers were considered good leavers by measure of their consistent performance. Out of the 28 people I reconnected with, 22 of them had gone on to succeed further in their careers—all owing to the moment they decided that their managers could no longer protect them from the culture that was evolving beyond what they were comfortable in.

Steve,[1] the Global Talent Acquisition Manager at a mobility startup, validated my findings. "It's true. I know it because we carried on being friends after and they admitted that leaving a place like ours was bittersweet, but they felt it was not the right place for them any longer. They had outgrown it. They just weren't enjoying it anymore. It wasn't something their direct manager could change."

As I sat down with a giant cup of coffee for our long overdue catch-up, I asked Steve ". . .so I remember you said leaving that company was a hard decision to make. Would you mind telling me why it was the right decision?"

---

[1]Steve is an interviewee of a tech startup in London who remains anonymous.

"Well, we were just acquired by this tech giant, and, granted, everyone was kind of shocked—why would I leave right now; I must have a lot of shares worth staying for. Well, after four years of working from the ground up with the Founder/CEO, he said to me, 'Steve, you don't have to stay if you don't want to, because I know you've been unhappy for a while. You are always challenging what the team wants, and we all know that as the acquisition starts to form there are going to be things that you won't agree with but that will be necessary. So, unless you get onboard now, it will be exceedingly difficult for you later. The people will change, the culture will as well, and I am far too busy getting the company to where it needs to be. In a way, we need a different you to be around.'"

He said that he was adamant it was the only way out of feeling trapped by his loyalty to the people he'd had the pleasure to work with for a quarter of a decade. Moving on was incredibly difficult for him, but soon enough, he found a new, early-stage startup to call home.

"Let's see how long I'll stay in this one before it starts to let me down," he smirked before we said goodbye.

A couple of years ago I realized I, too, was at a crossroads. I recalled how I tossed and turned, berating myself for wanting to resign from the safe haven that took me on after a cycle of burnouts from my last role. I had resigned and walked away from probably one of the best managers I have ever had. At that point in my life, I thought I was walking away from the height of my career. Vivid as day, I remember when David, my then manager, said, "I am saddened to hear that you did not come to me when you were struggling and that it's too late for me to do anything else to change your mind. This is a huge loss for us and for me." I was an early-stage employee, and I had played a part in shaping the culture of the startup.

I finally knew what it felt like for David. This must have been difficult to fathom because I was always open to talking about my struggles and challenges at work. He'd been the manager I would work hard to impress, and his encouragement meant everything to me. I wouldn't have been able to speak in public if it weren't for him. I wouldn't have learnt what recognition would mean for self-validation (which is all you need, by the way). I wouldn't have been brave enough to take on challenges at work and outside if it hadn't been for his belief in me. David did, in a lot of ways, shape my career even if I did not realize it at the time. He'd given me a voice when I was too afraid to use mine. I walked away from something I, too, was proud of putting together.

Staring at the data I had just collected, I let out a sigh of despair. As a manager, I thought that empowerment and autonomy were the things I should try to provide my team so they have the opportunity to carve out the career they feel most rewarding to them. Little did I know that by trying so hard to not block that endeavor, I had completely lost sight of the surroundings.

PEOPLE LEAVE COMPANIES, TOO, NOT JUST MANAGERS

So, the question is, why did I and so many others leave?

Over the years I have witnessed great people move on from great companies. Companies with a household brand that most people fight hard to get stamped on their CVs. The validation and recognition you would otherwise not obtain if you had not at least worked for them. But what happened to these great employees that they wanted to move on to do bigger, better things in life?

They move on because their managers don't always get to control the overall culture or environment in which they were thriving. While their managers are by their side, they get this thing called "air cover" around them that protects them from unpleasant interactions with other colleagues in the company. However as soon as they lose that bubble, the reality of a toxic culture surfaces, and their patience and hope starts to wane.

What happened was also the psychological consequences of great performers being affected by things they simply cannot control. This is what I mean by collateral damage. When your work starts to be less rewarding it is because the joy that used to fulfil you is now dampened by the strenuous daily battles of cultural misalignments. This is exceptionally detrimental to high performers as they carry on in life fulfilling themselves, not you, nor the company. These are people who know their self-worth, and will fight for what they believe is right, if not perfect, for them.

This was the case for Yasmin. I wasn't in control of the culture or the interactions she had to endure daily. Her colleagues were not supportive, and she often had to change her personality to fight for what she believed was right. This was a culture of individualists and she wasn't one. She was ambitious, but she was always protective of her team. As a manager, I was giving her "air cover" that felt protective but that detracted us from being able to establish better initiatives for the company. She began to realize that I wasn't going to be able to change these behaviors in every employee and our People team couldn't either.

Now, what happens if your manager is the CEO, or the founder of the organisation? Do you believe that things would be different from those in Chapter 3 when I talked about founders setting at least 80 percent of the culture? Well, in this case unfortunately, it is precisely the 20 percent left behind who the founder could not control. As companies go through growth, and especially in a startup where growth is all you focus on, you start to lose track of your founding principles at this point. Transparency and visibility turn into misunderstandings and misalignments because leaders no longer have time to talk through updates. Communication starts to lighten in frequency because a hierarchy now starts to form. "Thank yous" and "well dones" now form part of an official recognition framework, which is important to standardize in the growth stage, but completely kills the human element in working relationships.

There is also so much more at play now as the investor board becomes bigger, teams onboard new starters almost every week, and the people team grows too fast, so they are too busy to fix potholes left behind by tragically bad onboarding or neglected career developments caused by first-time managers. The startup begins to get overly crowded with non-trivial issues that just drains your day. And especially for an HR professional, this is a real kind of burn-out. These are such common startup issues that every article seems to talk about. But this is also the time we all forget about the well-being of our high performers.

How did that happen?

You probably did not realize it because we as managers/founders/ leaders start to take them for granted when we are busy ourselves. Because they were our deputies, we trusted them to take care of themselves. They have always been there for us, yet this is the time we begin to neglect their needs and their well-being. In the UK alone, more than 57 percent of employees feel psychological burnout from work and in total businesses in the country, pay an estimated £26 billion per annum in a combination of healthcare costs. No wonder mental health tech is rising in the country. Well done, startups.

In 2017, Eric Garton from *Harvard Business Review* mentioned that burn-out is not a personal problem, it is a company problem. Although the common reasons for this are weak time management and overloaded employees, one point he was leading toward was that high performers are loaded with the wrong attention at this stage. This is exactly what the employees are facing here caused by the lack of focus from the founders of the company.

Having investigated this phenomenon in multiple startups I have worked at, nine out of 10 high performers left in an emotionally burnt-out state. They go through a long cycle of trust, mistrust, trust, and mistrust until they realize they now have to take control of the situation themselves. As leaders, we all have our blind spots and often tell ourselves that they have outgrown us. Remember how I described the situation at the beginning of this chapter? That's what we do. As they left, we reflected and realized we'd actually let them down. It was our fault. If you are the manager, it's your fault. If you are the CEO, it's your fault. If you are the founder, it is your fault. They will never tell you this, but it is almost always your fault.

SOME, BUT NOT ALL, WOULD HAVE LEFT

"But why haven't they if it's as bad as it sounds?" I wondered. So, I asked them.

Over a virtual wine, I recently reconnected with a former colleague. Tony was my partner in crime. When I was in an early-stage startup, and it was scrappy working with ambiguity all the time, my ally, who understood it all, was the saving grace I needed to keep me sane. He was also the anchor to my volatility. Four years after I left, he was still there. Bear in mind that this person and I were on the same page because we cared for similar things, like the culture.

He is still there. He's still "sticking it out" as he calls it. Is he happy? Is he content? Does he feel fulfilled? No, and he regularly made it clear to me he is not. In the last few years, this became our thing where every three months or so we would catch up on life, and he would start and end with how dissatisfied he was with the decisions the leadership now makes (or always had, who knows by this point), and how he is no longer aligned with the direction of the company. He would list all the things he could not agree with and finally, "What I read from these recent Glassdoor reviews are also (almost) true." Distressed, he would sadly say, "We have changed. It's not the same company you knew. The founder had turned into a full-fledged narcissist who listen to no one but himself."

Indeed, the leadership team has had a total restructure and what that really meant was that all the founding partners had moved on. The company was now a new company, scaling up, with no familiar faces except for the few like Tony, who had been too afraid to leave because of personal circumstances. Personal circumstances meant there was no other job out there that would pay as well as this one. Tenure counts, right? So, that's one way to retain an employee.

Tony was one with personal circumstances. Judy on the other hand, is someone who still holds on hope that things will change one day. Let's call her Judy the Hopeful.

"How do you think it will be at this point?" I asked after listening to her ramble on about how unfairly treated she was because of nepotism. She had been waiting on a promotion that was promised yet got side-tracked because there was always another person who deserved it now, not later.

"Did you not raise this with the CEO, or did he just not do anything about it?" I asked, matching her exasperated tone.

"Honestly, I know the promotion will come. I am just not pushy enough, I guess, but he knows it. We talk about it over beers all the time. I have been with them four years now, and I know I am still an important asset to the business. Once I move up, it'll be down to me to remind him of the good old times when we were a company we could be proud of and from there, it will go back to how it used to be. I just have to be patient. I still believe in us," she said confidently, yet dispiritedly.

Unable to comprehend why both "Tony the Helpless" and "Judy the Hopeful" share similar conclusions even given their stark contrast in beliefs, I reached out to ask Bianca about the same. She had been there in the early days with me, and had been there for quite some time now, plus she was someone who would speak her mind if there was something bothering her. I thought I would at least hear her thoughts on how she is still finding joy in her work there.

Her first reaction was "Have you ever wondered what it'll be like to get out and be in a culture that you can at least have some control over?"

"Well, that's what I'm doing now," she continued. "I'm constantly fighting my way through to be in control of my own surroundings and that means I make sure the people I work with are okay. If they aren't, I just try to avoid them. It's not like our CEO doesn't know it. He has completely lost track of what's important to the company now. We're not 'his warriors' any longer, we're the 'people who work for him' now. You'd notice the difference if you were still around. I'm just waiting to leave once something good comes along. Trust me, they have no idea I'm looking elsewhere." True enough, she left a month after we had that conversation.

STAY ALERT BEFORE IT'S TOO LATE

As you are reading this and if you are the founder or CEO of your company, look around your startup and ask yourself, "How many of us from day one are still here?" Sure, you are probably still in contact and some of you may still be good friends because, again, these are your "good leavers." So, gather your courage, and ask them to validate this. Find out if they left because they felt helpless at some point, and you were not the person to save them from it. Find out why they walked away from something good (or at least you think so).

Ultimately this comes down to the founders.

Again, as you are reading this, find a way to have them remind you of what was important and how the company was formed with the foundation that you had all laid down together. Think back to the value they brought to build the brick and mortar of it. And hopefully you will be able to find a moment to connect back to the roots; not to remind you of how far you've come but to be reminded of the hard times you've gone through together.

Be mindful that if you don't act early enough, you will lose your loyal soldiers. Early-stage employees don't necessarily share the same traits as late-stage employees because they believed in your mission when it was merely an idea. They were part of those late-night round-table discussions. They were the ones who brought on some of their trusted friends to help make your dreams come true. Also, don't forget they also probably sacrificed monetarily to just get this engine cranked up and started. If you are not addressing this immediately, they will continue to battle this cultural misfit every day.

As I close this chapter, I am overwhelmed with a sense of guilt. If there were one thing I could have done differently to retain Yasmin, it would have been to try harder at changing the culture from the top and to champion the principle enough to have made her day-to-day more fulfilling than simply solving other people's problems. I would have tried my best to solve her problem because it was my problem to fix.

So, founders, don't lose track of what was important then and what is still important now.

CHAPTER 5

The Unlearner

Every startup was born from an idea to solve something that isn't working right now in our world. It's natural to believe that the startup was born from the frustration of a founder to create a solution that doesn't quite exist yet. If you've ever been in a room with enough founders, you'll know that the majority of them are 80 percent frustrated and 20 percent excited.

It doesn't matter if they're in an accelerator (to help a startup with scaling up and growth) or an incubator (to help founding teams' disruptive ideas with the hope of building out a business model and company). Their anxiety is evident to me.

Not all founders are leaders in armor rising from the ground to bring us answers the world doesn't know are needed. Not all founders are the same shape. Some have never done this before, let alone are leaders or managers in their lives.

Some have spent most of their last decade or two being managers and executives, fulfilling someone else's dreams. So, now it is their turn to realize their dreams, vowing to be better managers than those duds they were just reporting to a month ago. I call these new founders corporate hackers.

This is a polite way to describe them, but another slightly more discourteous way of describing them would be to call them the Unlearners. Individuals who have lived in frustration with others have found a way to redefine themselves to compensate for what they couldn't have in their last positions. They go into redemption mode from day one, and we've watched them succeed in breaking the legacy mold and sometimes lose sight of their purpose.

How many founders were already millionaires before their startup became successful? How many successful entrepreneurs do we know who had mom and dad's help at the beginning? I'm thinking about Jeff Bezos, Elon Musk, Bill Gates, and how Mark Zuckerberg had borrowed not a small sum from his father to launch Facebook. Or Michael Dell, who openly credits his parents when they offered some seed money for his fledgling computer business at the time.

When I started my research on this topic, a popular view was about the millenarian controversy of Kylie Jenner.

As an American media personality, socialite, model, and business-woman, she is also the founder and owner of cosmetic company Kylie Cosmetics, sold to Coty Inc. in 2019 for $600 million for a majority stake in her company. With this, she was propelled into *Forbes's* list of the newest self-made billionaire in early 2020, only to receive a backlash of disagreements.

The people did not believe Kylie was self-made. She eventually got booted off the list as soon as the Spring of that year. The debate questioned whether her money could be considered "self-made" if she came from such a privileged background. Naturally, she defended and claimed that her parents cut her off at the age of 15 when she started making her fortune using the platform she created for herself. She continued to argue that she inherited none of her money when being recognized by *Forbes*.

So, which one is it? I honestly don't know.

But what I do know is that whether founders had a fortune before they started their new startup will make a difference. I have had the opportunity to meet founders who would go on and build mediocre companies with an Okay brand, Okay product, and often stayed behind the limelight even if they tried differently, although never hard enough. And the reason for this is because of these "hands-off CEOs" who are not hungry enough to trailblaze their mission.

The pattern is pretty obvious if you have watched the evolution of some of these Okay companies.

First, they carry a misperception of being bootstrap. Bootstrapping a business is when an entrepreneur/founder starts a self-sustaining business and grows it while using limited resources or money. This is accomplished most times without the use of venture capital firms or even a significant angel investment.

As difficult as it sounds, we have seen some of the most prominent startups revolutionize their solutions. Look at **Canva**, an online design and publishing tool for anyone without designer skills. Canva is well known in Australia for its bootstrapping success in the earlier days.

Or **11:FS** in the UK, a digital financial services firm, was building innovative solutions for present banks. However, bootstrap meant they didn't need to go out into the competitive capital market to raise the funds they needed because they usually have a pretty good, lucrative opening at the very start.

COMPANY A

"We have a family office investing in us, and it's pretty much a cash cow. We will be fine for a while."

Candidates coming out of these companies often reveal that they're looking for new jobs because the companies aren't forward-thinking enough.

"By the sounds of it, the culture seems to be pretty calm while most people in startups are heavily under stress, which drives them out of the company. So, tell me, really, why are you looking to leave?"

"Since you've asked, I've been hired to launch new products, but as you must have seen, we have not launched anything new for a couple of years now. I am ready to move on. It's affecting my career."

"Why is that so? Is it because of the lack of talent to help you? Can I help you build your team?" the opportunist in me asked. As an agency recruiter at that time, any indirect business was a big win for me.

"Actually, it's not the team. The CEO changes his mind all the time about what we should be doing, and we just ended up wasting a lot of time not starting anything. Plus, there is quite a bit of backup money, so it's not like we're desperate or in a rush to prove ourselves. Nothing like that at all. That's why I figured even in the next three years, I won't be mounting anything new."

This was Max, a senior executive in a London-based Credit Fin-Tech who had been with the company for about three years, willing to entertain a role with a bump down in salary just so that he could get out of this mundane, lackluster progress of a career.

As their Vice President of Product, he felt he was sold the dream to launch new products because of the ambitions of the CEO when he interviewed with them. They didn't lowball his asking salary and could meet all the requests he'd asked for, albeit their being in the early stage. He had walked out of a high street bank into an eight-month-old startup with the same package as before. He thought he had hit the jackpot.

"I was very interested in the startup scene, but the problem was always around what they couldn't afford. You know what they say, right? That going into a startup means you get more equity than salary, but equity is just as risky on its own. So, for me, getting an offer like that, including a bump up in my title, I thought this was it. This was my opportunity without any risks, right?"

"Plus, there weren't any red flags at all during the whole hiring process."

This is another problem. Because these companies often do not have anything terrible to show, their interview process is usually relatively smooth with almost no red flags. The culture there is generally quite calm as people wouldn't be over-stressed with impending deadlines every 48 hours.

Their goals remain the same throughout the year with little to no variations, which allows their employees to work just core hours and they would have never been penalized for not achieving some targets. To Max, this company didn't hear much from their CEO except when it was a PR situation.

They have a hands-off CEO who stepped back from the day-to-day activities to focus on propagating the business. A lot of times, this is essential for growth to avoid a micro-managing situation. Except this CEO was mainly distracted and lost focus on the goals. According to Max, the CEO had not set any new directions for over a year.

"It was just an unfortunate situation, which I believe was driven by the lack of purpose altogether." He wrapped up before I decided to carry on interviewing him for another position in a different FinTech.

In my experience, you don't learn by being in the company but from the people desperate to leave it, especially these senior managers, which leads us to Adrian.

COMPANY B

Adrian describes this startup as having a critical mission to bring banking to the underserved in the European market. This idea refers to adults who either do not use or do not have access to any traditional financial services, including savings accounts and credit cards readily available to most people. This lack of adequate financial services is due to their social and economic background.

They were meant to be creating a solution to help those that had ignored high street banks. The goal was to bring some equality back to their lives. While the company held on to this imperative duty, they didn't hold on to it long enough because of the Founder/CEO.

Like some founders that had an early successful start in their corporate lives, Mr. Vanilla bootstrapped the company with his plus family capital. This was meant to be a sweet spot for any startup because, first, they had a clear purpose. Second, they had an excellent, well-experienced team. Third, there was an abundance of customers in need of this service. Fourth, their CEO was an all-around good person, hence the purpose, right? And fifth, they had the privilege to make any mistakes without costing the business at all.

It was a recipe for ultimate success. All of this would have meant an incredibly smooth path by expectation, except that Mr. Vanilla was just "meh" in every way. It was just ordinary.

This was also why Adrian left one of the fastest-growing startups to join them. Adrian had been with them for a few years before we met the first time at a FinTech conference. As any usual introductions go, he asked me if the company I was working for, another FinTech, would be interested in hiring someone "with his profile."

As he dove deeper into the conversation, I realized he was on the verge of calling it quits every other day. He felt this way because there was absolutely no involvement, motivation, or even just sheer energy to make any improvements in their product. This lack of interest was infesting the leadership team, including the CEO. At this point, I was confused.

I asked, "Why? Does the app work? I knew of people who were using it. Has the app changed their lives?"

Adrian revealed to me, "Of course it works. We've been at it for years, and I know it works. Unless you're also a customer of ours, you won't know that it only works to a certain point. All they can do now is store their money with us like they would with any other bank and nothing more. We would do so much better if we were true to our mission. Right now, it is a far cry from it."

He continued, "I work with our customers every day, I get all this feedback, but it goes nowhere. Whenever I push the top team to consider changing or improving things, as pointed out so clearly by our customers, they say, 'It's fine. If it isn't broken, don't fix it.'"

"Ah, so you have a corporate culture then?" I asked.

"When you put it that way, yes, sadly. And it turned quickly into that too. It's the most familiar thing to everyone on the leadership team. It's what they know and what they're only willing to work with."

"Right," I said. "I get it. And you don't think you could ever get through to your CEO? I mean, like maybe shake him up a little? What about your competition!?"

"We haven't got much competition, that's why. But even if we do suddenly, we would be their breakfast overnight. That's how bad things are."

"Okay, let me get this straight," I tried to understand. "Is it bad for YOU, or everyone?"

"Bad for me, I guess. . .everyone else seems to be fine with this. No pressure at work sounds a bit like a dream for most people, I guess. . ."

As a startup that has been around for over six years, albeit never making any positive revenue, they had never been known to raise any round of capital. Yet, they seemed to stay in the background with a bit of limelight on them. I finally understood why I never talked about them either.

"We're lacking personalities. And no one here has a passion. I don't know how I've lasted three years, to be honest. It's bizarre we're still standing." He could have said out of major frustration, but can you blame him?

Adrian left shortly after our conversation that day. Over the years, I had kept a close eye on his career. He worked with some of the more prominent startups around the globe. There are several significant product launches with his name on them.

The company he left announced its first round of fundraising earlier this year (2021). It was also rumored they were discussing partnering with a local infrastructure company. This marriage would expand their product beyond banking. They were also exploring credit as an extension to their customers: new direction, same CEO.

"Can we teach an old dog a new trick? I'm not sure. . ." Those were the last words Adrian left me to ponder.

COMPANY C

Now let's talk about another company that proved an overhaul sometimes isn't a bad thing, especially when it starts to feel quite stuck.

An ex-banker founded this startup. A high-profiled person, too. Its start was inevitably a smooth sailing journey with a good-sized capital to kick off its launch. Their offering was not ordinary, but it was one in a market not yet saturated by demands, ergo, not yet enough competitors.

As the years went by, the startup matured with off-the-mill resignations. They had new hiring campaigns every six months and provided business banking services to small businesses as an alternative to the big banks. Again, nothing they wouldn't do that wasn't what they'd been doing so far.

Demand increased, and competitors crept upon them, delivering the same if not far more superior services for half the cost and time. This was a personal experience for me as I was a customer who moved on to their competitors because I was getting the same quality of service year in year out with slight variation to offer.

I recalled asking the customer agent for a slightly challenging request only to be met with a refusal and the comment, "I thought you're a startup? Can't you get creative to solve my problem?"

I also remember letting off steam at the agent that day. It was also the day I became a customer of their competitor.

A little over two years later, I was a host in a panel discussion, and one of the guests was the Vice President of Company Two. It was a discussion about the competitive landscape that business banking had become.

This discussion was also an opportunity to celebrate the promotion of this VP as their new CEO was "taking the company into new directions, exploring beyond business banking." This news came when the Founder/CEO, was naturally moving into a chairman role after ten years of being in position and finally deciding to pass the baton down to the next in line.

"What are you most excited about coming into this new role? And what does it mean for the company?" I asked.

"Everything about it! Hopefully, it'll mean a new culture as we break down our old walls and serve our customers as we should have a while ago. They want more, and we're going to deliver just that. We will be bringing in new teams, and we're excited about all of these changes."

The new CEO was not wrong at all, it seemed. In the last two years, I have heard their name more times than I remembered, and their new Head of Marketing had gone on to be recognized as one of the rising stars in FinTech. The company had embraced their desperately needed overhaul to the extent of changing the brand's name and mission altogether. They announced that they raised new capital in late 2019 and had since seen talent racing to get into the company. They were finally noted as competitive.

COMPANY D,E,F. . . (OR MAYBE MORE)

What if there was a Founder/CEO who is just unwilling to learn new ways of working even though everyone around them tells them so? Or a stubborn CEO who says they want things to change simultaneously and thinks it does not apply to them?

This was a startup with a founder who usually had pretty mild behaviors, which meant you would not have an anxiety attack if your proposal for a new feature wasn't ground-breaking. He would probably say something like, "Okay, it looks good but let's try a different color, I guess."

They often don't show a sense of urgency in their attitude and create a safe and harmonious culture for the outsider. Still, their employees get incredibly bored and probably only held on to their jobs because it was easier. This company saw their competitors and the world slip by them but didn't get to a point to wake up from this dream until they started running out of money. For some, it also became too late.

They also have an obvious trend when it comes to their hiring. If at this point you already have a company in mind that reminds you of this, reflect on their earlier management team when they had just started. They usually come from a senior background, have been working in the industry if not a similar product for a long time, and always come with a hefty salary even when the company is probably only under 20 employees.

It is infrequent for successful startups to afford this type of salary as early as this. From my experience, there were two main reasons they did this. Hiring the right talent would open more business opportunities, but the more senior, the better. Senior hires are typically well-established.

AND

These talents would not sacrifice their previous salaries for a startup, so they sacrificed their mission instead.

As I interviewed **Jon Fernandez**, a Talent Acquisition expert in the European market for some of the biggest and hottest Tech Start-ups, he weighed in on the impact of a startup without a strong ambition toward potential candidates.

You have worked for some of the biggest names in the current market. What I'm most interested in is that when a company doesn't show a goal-oriented or ambition-driven culture, what happens to candidates you interview for their roles?

"Most of the time, they will not end up working at these organizations. Or worse, these organizations will end up hiring under qualified candidates because they find themselves with a shortage of talent interested in their company. Once the company has a reputation, it will be hard to revert that. Let me put it this way, candidates going for roles without ambition end up 1. Withdrawing their application at some point, 2. Trying to get a 'just in case' offer while they are interviewing elsewhere, 3. Will

not join the company, simply, or 4. Will join the company but then leave after a very short period of time.

"The last company I was at briefly, Oxsed (a UK biotech startup) went through this exact churn of candidates. After a quick few months of gaining that reputation, we couldn't even attract any candidates let alone, good ones."

Why do you think low ambition means that fewer quality hires will enter the company?

"When a company doesn't show ambition, it will end up attracting the same type of candidates. This translates to employees who will not bring value to the existing teams, will not run the extra mile, and not challenge the status quo. They will be clocking in at 9 a.m. and out at 6 p.m. They aren't interested in developing their career and are sometimes driven to find ways to work less."

I also noticed that you were previously an agency recruiter. Is it easier or harder to source and fill roles in these companies?

"Similar, to be honest."

Why?

"There are lots of differences between In-house and Agency recruiter, but let's go with the main one. Which is that, here, companies had to pay a fee, but they will be desperate to hire someone for their positions, and I will struggle to find a suitable candidate that would work with them.

Sourcing and finding candidates were the easy parts. The hard part was, 'how do I sell this role to this great candidate who could get a job in a much, much better company?'

"I was lucky enough to work in an agency that believed in good and ethical hiring practices, so I focused on finding strong candidates with great experience or skills and, most importantly, AMBITIOUS for these organizations. But I learned quickly that ambitious candidates end up working or accepting offers from ambitious companies all the time. Which made me realize that I had to be more conscious on how I would match what a candidate is looking for in a role and company."

What about their leavers? What is the usual reason they give you coming out of these companies?

"They are normally very diplomatic when they speak about the reasons for leaving but the most common ones are 1. poor culture, 2. misalignment of role, 3. poor leadership or management, and 4. lack of career progression, which all stems from having no clear ambitions from the start."

THE WILLINGNESS TO LEARN FROM EXPERIENCE

PAYDOCK (FinTech)

Not all things are bad when you have an experienced Founder/CEO who knows what they want to deliver and bring the company on the right journey. Take **Paydock**, for example. A newly founded startup that began in Australia and expanded its operation in Europe.

Even at their early stage, Paydock is already taking strides in winning some of the coveted Financial Services and Tech awards in both regions. Speaking to **Suzanne Piddock**, their Head of Operations in London, I learned their secret to harnessing these past learnings and experiences. Simply put, we talked about how an experienced Founder and CEO showed more resilience than one who isn't.

You've been with Paydock since the early days and have seen the company's evolution. Can you tell me more about the

company's founder, Rob? Did you feel his experience made a difference?

"Of course. I've worked with startups in the past where there had been inexperienced CEOs and inexperienced founders. You don't usually get this combination of experience here in a startup. So yes, that for me was a massive draw. Resilience is another attribute I found myself witnessing in this company, in the leadership team. As a founder and my manager, Rob was really transparent with me from the start. He told me about all these issues that he'd had in the past company, and because of that, he said to me, 'This is why I wanted to meet you face to face because culture and value alignment has to be at the core of what we do now.'

"He said, 'I'm trying to build it the right way now, and that has to be the foundation because that's what was missing before. It's important to all of us here.'

"So, 100 percent I think he brings that to the table and it's reassuring for people as well. Obviously, like other startups, we are still learning. But I do believe that people are really forgiving of that kind of unstructured way of working early on because of Rob's drive and motivation.

"I guess all founders have that, but it's about how they use it to bring everyone on the journey with them. That's the kind of driving factor that I think of even when we have to tell unwelcome news to the employees (and it's never always smooth sailing). Every company will have times in which tough news has to be delivered, while there is a way we can say 'this is common to all' but how we get through it is something we want to focus on. Turning a challenging time into a very special memory of pulling in together. At any other company, you would expect it to be an uproar, but it didn't happen to us. Instead, when we had challenging times, everyone else just raised their hands to offer their support. That is our culture. We're strong on making sure we can pitch in and help each other out. We wanted to do what we can to keep everything going during a difficult time."

She certainly wasn't wrong. Over the few months I worked with them, I witnessed how having a founder who holds the culture close to heart makes a difference in getting through typical growing pains, much less challenging (or painful). I think that's a true testament, from how strongly Rob felt about setting the right foundation as the leadership team also try to balance that with building a highly accountable, high-performance culture that still always comes down on the side of kindness, respect, and vision for individual capacity in a company that does not necessarily conflict with performance.

The difference here was evident—separated between emergent and deliberate strategies. While the other Founder/CEOs were deliberately maintaining their status quo of who they only wanted to be, this CEO was doing what he needed to do to take the company forward successfully.

WHAT IF EXPERIENCED FOUNDERS FORGOT THEY ARE ALSO ON A LEARNING JOURNEY?

Lori has not only worked for experienced founders in multiple start-ups, but she has also been an ardent pre/seed investor for over a decade now. As I recognize that her learnings were crucial to validating some of my opinions, we caught up on one of her most challenging times working with the founding team of another startup.

Freeup was an early-stage FinTech acquired by Greensil in early 2019, which many might describe as successful because they had a rare early exit. However, looking back at it, she felt gutted that they didn't achieve their full potential via the exit. And this had everything to do with recognizing that even as experienced founders, there were still things that needed learning.

"It started as a great opportunity for us to sort of take a shortcut, attach ourselves to a bigger corporation, and see the potential magnitude of our growth overnight. We're talking about going from 8 to 200 clients in a short time."

It was a rare chance to propel the company, but it quickly burnt out their culture as it just didn't manage to settle into the corporation. "Losing our WHY, our independence, and suddenly becoming a department rather than an arm of a partner" was how she said she reasoned with it. As experienced founders already at the time, they had underestimated the continued learning needs.

"I think at some point, none of us really understood what we were expecting. If we had gone with more advice from others who had done this before, the company would look very different now. We were becoming a department that wasn't the driver of the larger business, so we had things we had to consistently fight for. These were the same things we took for granted when we were a startup. At the same time, though, you can particularly argue that you now have unlimited resources as well, and it's kind of like a nice cushion choice.

"It was an uncommon problem for most founders if you were asked to make a hard choice between having a VC (venture capitalist) to back you up versus a large corporation to acquire you. I think anyone given those options would choose the easier route unless they've done it before and didn't like how it turned out after. At the end of the day, being a founder means deciding to sell your business or not. Simple as that."

One thing that stayed with me after we parted ways that day was how she felt guilty for having a blind spot that ignored the red flags during the acquisition just because the team thought they were experienced already.

"We should have never stopped learning." As she carried on describing how on the day of signing themselves over to Greensil there were four of their founding team on one side and a whole 30-person legal team on the other side. "Being inexperienced, we didn't ask questions that were fundamental, crucial for future alignment, or even considering if their vision to our business forward was the right one for everyone.

"On the flip side, we had learned so much from the process, which we otherwise would not have had the exposure to. As an investor, it also opened my eyes to what to look for in founders or even a founding team to be honest. Being able to find out if a startup has the right structure and governance framework or strategy to move forward is the first thing I look for now in most startups. Let's just put it this way; there are founders who are still learning and those who stopped learning. Guess which ones I pick?"

As far as these real stories from real people go, the good and the bad co-exist in our realities. But the ones that I'm a little unsure about are those who don't show a lot of over-ambition and therefore end up having a mild behavior that sometimes works for the company and sometimes just doesn't. Do you agree?

These are startups that turn into a Unicorn or beyond by doing things at a pace. You find them climbing to the top, usually in a steady state when done right. Well, it's a balance. Some of them turn out well, and some not so much.

In Chapter 6, we will look at the complete opposite of an Unlearner, one devoted to their mission and passionate about their goals. That is until the over obsession turns them into a micro-manager that is a dangerous version of a hands-on CEO.

CHAPTER 6

The Trailblazer

As in Chapter 5, some people are still desperate to break themselves out of a stereotypical label of being called "old school" or "too old to try." So, they end up focusing on making sure they have risen above their past and creating a company that is nothing like before. While some of the more self-aware founders (although not innate to all founders) become the Trailblazer type, the ones largely lacking in this department become leaders that create toxic, dysfunctional cultures.

We have always associated them with founders who have creative problem-solving skills, are charismatic enough for you to embrace their new ideas, and most incredibly, adapt to new environments. Except when this person wants to break the mold, and they forget what it was like to be a good manager.

THE SHINY SIDE OF THE COIN

Entrepreneurs are expected to be the person (or people) willing to take risks and go into a path that isn't already there. Sometimes they are also called pioneers, but the sheer difference here is that they would not just stop at being a groundbreaker but also set a trail and leave a new path for others to follow. We have called them innovators, or even people who discover something new and make it acceptable in society as if it had always been there. That's how good they are.

Once, I met a serial entrepreneur at a surf camp while he explained why he had used surfing as a metaphor for life. He said, "When someone is surfing, they have no control over the waves, so the waves will come and go regardless of what they wanted to do. It's the same as being a founder in a lot of ways. I can plan as best as I can, but it will always catch me by surprise, so I'm learning every day. Every startup I've gone through, they all taught me what to avoid next." I didn't realize how true that was until we reconnected while writing this.

Some of the world's renowned trailblazers include Sara Blakely, the creator of Spanx. Tony Fadell of Nest Labs and Miri Ratner, who co-founded Yayar. Spanx brought about a need for garments to shape our bodies. Nest labs created "learning thermostats" for easy self-installation, and Yayar developed early detection for breast cancer and applied the same technology into day-to-day things like security systems. Just to name a few, of course.

During the era of my career, I have been fortunate enough to be part of a startup set up by four pioneering founders who were ex-corporates themselves but vowed daily to create a company they would be proud of, not scornful of.

David, the CEO, had in mind a company brand that would be the *Google of Consulting*, ground-breaking, not contend with politics, and their employees or alumni would wear their experience like a badge of honor. I still do to this day since I started with the company in 2017.

I spoke to **Ross Methven**, who was the other founder of 11:FS. He had a largely distinctive leadership style focused on creating family-like, close-knit team dynamics. He weighed in on why the company needed to design the change they wanted to see.

What has it been like for you to build a company with a culture known as it is?

"I think part of the reason for success has been the autonomy that we've given people. They're told to not be afraid to ask but we also genuinely meant that. It wasn't a textbook management style. Even from quite early on, anybody in the company with a good idea or something encouraged a discussion over them. We made sure there was never any politics or artificial hierarchies going on, where everybody had an equal voice, which has been a really important part of the culture. And that's the thing that can sometimes be a bit harder to hold onto as you try and scale the business while adding more people. As you add more layers, there's a risk of that disappearing. So, listening and giving people autonomy has been important for us."

Did you have to draw from past experiences?

"So, let's glimpse back to my past. The first job I had out of university was working for a company where there was literally the company owner, a secretary, me, and a fax machine. Simple, but if it was in line with what the business was trying to achieve, and

it was a good idea, you didn't even have to ask permission. You just went ahead and delivered, and I find that I love that. And it just suited me as an individual, but I could also see the benefits of bringing it into the business as well. And because I enjoyed that sort of environment and thrived, I think it's something even today that I still do. I've just had a couple of key meetings this morning to address some business problems we're trying to solve. We just kind of put them out there, and anybody can come up with suggestions. This was how we solved big problems in the past. That shows by encouraging people to speak up, allowing your teams to access them, we all benefit from it. That's something that has always been an important part of 11:FS, and I think it makes everybody feel involved and empowered."

I think it's essential for people to feel like they belong and are part of your journey. To me, 11:FS feels like it is a business of people.

"Absolutely. A lot of the repeat business we get comes from relationships that have been developed. Yes, we've got very good products and services, but they're all essentially delivered by people or account managers. So really, it's all off the back of relationships. I think it's particularly important for a startup because when it is all new, you don't have a track record or decades of performance to rely on. Developing our relationships is so important because to start with, we're not like McKinsey or a sort of a well-established consulting firm where people already have relationships with the brand. People had no relationship with our brand. So, it had to be led by the people."

Finally, I have one fundamental question. 11:FS is lucky to have four co-founders. Most companies have one sole person that decides everything. Did you feel that was a plus for the company?

"Yes, absolutely. I also think David (the CEO) did a great job assembling the people he did because we were all quite different

yet complementary. We have different backgrounds, experiences, and values we bring to the table. In the early days, sales were so important and we had to bring in revenue, so you'll see us doing that together regardless of who you were or what your job or specialty was. To get this company up off the ground, this is what we used to do together. And then as the company matured and evolved, we became more complex. Our differences came back into play and we've been leading in our expert areas since. For example, we've got Simon with the experience of working in big banks, and because they're our customers, he understands their culture and ways of working. And Jason's very much a guru in the FinTech environment, which also helps us. So, I think it's important to have you know, not just the complementary experiences, but also the mix of personalities and leadership styles that gives us completely different ways of thinking. But I know what you're thinking, how different can four white guys be, right? We're actually all quite different."

Yes, I think I think so too.

"I remember the times when we started to get a little bit more complex, we also made a huge effort to diversify the group and we got to a point where we had a really strong leadership team. The people came from completely different backgrounds, not just based on what the business need was at that time, but also because we're bringing in diverse minds rather than just looking at okay, we've got four white guys.

Even after three long years have passed since I said goodbye to the teams, it was comforting to know that when founders start out doing the right thing in building their companies, they usually don't veer off tangent and forget why they did this in the first place. After a short exchange with Rachel,[1] Business Manager of

---

[1] Rachel is a former employee interviewed who remains anonymous.

the company who had been there since their early days, she con-
firmed my suspicions.

Of course, we evolved over time, and each time it gets a little
harder, but it's also very rewarding to see that we haven't forgotten
who we are and what we care about. The founders stayed com-
mitted to our purpose, and I genuinely think this is the reason we
haven't felt lost like you know some startups do. After a few years,
you just hear a totally different tone, see different personalities,
and become a different thing altogether. For us, the services may
have diversified, and the people have grown or left. I still feel I
belong after these years. So, it counts for something for sure."

When done right, it creates a harmonious working environment and a transparent and consistent culture. This is due to the focus that doesn't change over time and makes actual concise and consistent communications. Members of the executives, managers, and employees hardly feel overwhelmed with non-filtered communication from the top that is easy to digest and act on.

Companies with a dearth of strategic updates from their leadership or CEO would often get confused as they seem to look like free ideas that are difficult to trail and comprehend. More often than not, CEOs are then encouraged to raise as a single voice, which leads to stifling the autonomy that was once created to encourage a better culture.

There is also the element of creating and cultivating more effective managers in this environment as they would be idiosyncratically focused on execution. When founders forget that their employees are responsible for their people, they are forced to be individual contributors due to time constraints. And they deliver pressures inflicted on them from the inconsistency of demands from a CEO unwilling to learn new ways of working. Managers should be left to execute while enjoying managing, coaching, and mentoring their teams because as their team wins, the whole company wins.

THE OTHER SIDE OF THE COIN

Ego is probably a strength in most entrepreneurs (or so I've heard enough founders praising themselves for this trait). It's beneficial in ways to go from ideas to building a product and pick themselves up when it fails. But sometimes, we meet (unfortunately) founders that let their past successes become their demons. They display sheer delusional arrogance made of their impulsive behavior biased towards unplanned actions. They fear failure and catastrophically their self-doubt. These are the ones you recall having a mere discussion with about a topic in *your* expertize only to find yourself walking out of that office losing the battle because your CEO simply would not listen to anyone but their intentions.

There are many reasons why some startups fail. Egotistical founders would blame their failures on the shortcomings of others, or point fingers at events out of their control. At the same time, as they are trying to break the mold in this new startup, they lose track of needing change while they primarily focus on a similar reflection, one they are familiar with already.

Then comes their lack of self-awareness.

Bruno, my CFO, stormed into the office that morning and let out a loud sigh. I saw exasperation in his face like I had not seen before and thought to myself, "What could have possibly happened that would annoy this well-tempered man?" I should have given him some space to calm before I approached him.

As my trusted confidante, my suspicions were correct. It had reached a breaking point in his relationship with our CEO where he had felt let down by the person he should be looking up to for directions. Lucas, our CEO, had been known for his compulsive decision-making process, and the aftermath had not always been pretty. It would cause a string of departures, both senior and junior levels, but the one thing we had was our CFO, who would also be able to step back in to recoup what he could. Except at this point, he felt his time of fixing was up.

"Are you sure there's nothing else we can do to change his mind? You have explained that this is for the good of the business, yes?" I started over a shared pot of calming tea.

"Of course, I did. I always do. And truth be told, I haven't been at my best because this constant battle of proving a point started to wear me down a few months ago. I have been patient, seeing that we have a lot of employees at stake. But this isn't the job I signed up for, not his coach that he doesn't listen to, no," he explained in frustration. I could see the exhaustion in his eyes as we continued to discuss the issue.

"To put things into context, this wasn't about a 'do or die' for the company type of situation. This was about deciding to disburse bonuses for the employees. We were close to the end of the fiscal year. It seemed nontrivial at the time, except Bruno had learned how unreasonable Lucas had been over the last two years.

"He's drinking his own Kool-Aid, honestly. This has been a tough year for everyone, so they absolutely do deserve this bonus, even if it might not seem life changing. He is unable to listen to anything the group had put together over the last month. My biggest issue here is when he said, 'People need jobs so they will stay even without this. We don't need to overdo it. I will convince them if you can't.' Which you know he will, eventually."

I heard his fear, and I knew exactly what he meant. Lucas is undoubtedly an intelligent person, credible in the company for founding the business, and an incredibly influential founder who sometimes uses that skill with the wrong intentions. Have you ever gone through a moment when you walk in to discuss one thing and leave the room with an answer you didn't expect, satisfied, only to then get quickly hit by the truth that you actually did not at all solve that problem? And you are most definitely back to square one? Yes, that's exactly how it feels to go into any discussion with Lucas. His go-to leadership style is to mildly dismiss your opinions so that we can get back on track to what he wants us to do instead. Any topic of discussion not inherently raised by him is not up for debate at all. His company comes first, so do his instructions.

As CEOs show these behaviors, they also, unfortunately, create a toxic, dysfunctional environment where no one thrives (or sticks around) long enough for the company to be splendidly successful. They make highly inefficient companies with multitudes of issues that stem from leadership and an environment plagued with unsafe, unhappy employees. Let's have a look at the common consequences, which perhaps you may be familiar with.

LACK OF SAFETY TO FAIL

They use it as a stick or excuse to blame the people on the hook for deliverables, even though they don't have the tools or resources to get it done well or sometimes at all. As the leadership team or CEO is far away from the on-the-ground scenario, they do not always know how difficult some tasks are to start, let alone complete. For example, the team may be asked to generate more and more reports when the intelligence infrastructure has not been set up to deliver their reports. When these affected teams expand their workload to support time constraints, they only find their other priorities imploding because the CEO asked for a "this needs to be tracked, get it done" project.

"Things are tough down here," is what my team would tell you, confessed the Head of Engineering at his exit interview. "For example, I was constantly punished when a failure happened due to product negligence and a decision to release without testing or rollout monitoring in place. I have heard it being used differently on me several times to take the team's freedom away as they are now seen as unable to make the right call for action. We were never set up to make any decisions except to heel."

LACK OF CO-CREATION OF STRATEGIES

Like the way the CEO sets strategy and priorities becomes unclear. The management layers begin to question the "why" and the "what" and assume their part in executing these goals. A closer look shows that the lack of intent to co-create with its management on its strategy, departments, functions, and teams caused it to naturally become a "just do it because I said so," and "there are consequences if you fail" pattern.

The danger here is if the strategy itself was not well-formed initially or never agreed upon, communication will take the form of "get this done or else," and often comes with a "this is a non-negotiable" sub-clause. This leads directly to employees working extra hours to show progress against those requirements, rather than having a healthy discourse around what is required.

"A more meaningful outcome of the work would come if the CEO would focus less on things that just needed to be done and take us on his journey. Tell us where we're heading, and maybe we will enjoy this more. . . ," one burnt-out engineer once told me.

"When information did come to the engineering team about the results of the strategy sessions apparently done by just the CEO, it was in the form of a not-very-well-formed plan. However, the fact that the plan wasn't well-formed was not the issue. The issue here was the strategy and the rationale behind the plan were not communicated at all—the plan was simply presented. This approach feels like a 'do as you're told' rather than a 'let's do this together.' The former approach leads to frustration, stress, and burnout while the latter is empowering and energizing. Couple that with a little bit of autonomy within the teams, and we can make meaningful improvements rather than just reacting to crises," said the engineer as he departed us only about a week later.

PEOPLE ARE CONSTANTLY TOLD WHAT AND HOW TO DO THEIR JOBS

Although we preach that we want objective-focused teams, 90 percent of our conversations seem to be at the task and list level. This approach itself hinders the learning and growth of the people, not to mention how it adds pressure to them, which subsequently puts the work at risk. Employees get told off when work doesn't get done in the same way the CEO requested. This was a strong sign of control and micro-management in a culture that is fearful of its leader. As a startup that was supposed to be breaking corporate world barriers, we seemed to be big on the anti-self-organization behavior.

While I had facilitated the Analysis Planning for the team, the team was silent at specific times, listening to the CEO telling them how they should be conducting analysis and the steps they should follow. Managers close to the CEO would also learn to mimic this behavior as a way of success. Or they acted in that way to get valida-tion for their position in the company. So, the apple doesn't tend to fall far from the tree.

For example, on more than one occasion, I have sat next to a UX designer and listened to a product person telling them how to do their job very explicitly, even without a direct reporting line that may have excused that behavior. This designer was being told to go to other com-panies to find out what they were doing and seek to replicate it; other-wise, it would be a failure in their terms. When asked if the managers needed to check every single line of code in the team because it was a non-sustainable way of working, I was met with a firm "Yes, we have to do this because I am the manager."

A short-lived coach wrote the following suggestion in his report before he decided this was a place that would not change unless the CEO did. "Move the conversations to an objective level and help peo-ple set clear and time bound objectives and provide the freedom and support to allow them to go after them. For example, learn to 'Build a process and flow that focuses on analysis, to derive customer insights and feed the engineering of value to customers.'"

One of our Chief Product Officers worked hard until it was time for exit, caused by many unnerving micromanagement situations. It paralysed his ability to perform. When it got too much to handle, we had a discussion.

How would you describe the CEO's leadership style?

"I think he's a visionary who is constantly exploring and pushing the limits of what you can envision. The negative is if you end up

exploring too much out of normal pace you lose sight of very interesting solutions too. Not to mention the rest of the team has to play catch up to the fast mind of the CEO. So, what happens is that we have a brilliant CEO whose mind runs at 10,000km per second and it's a constant struggle to keep up with and to define a consistent project."

Why do you think it has led him to being a micromanager?

"I think it's frustration on his side that we couldn't keep up his pace, basically. Be on the same trajectory as he was, and he wants to ensure that he could place us in the right direction."

Do you agree that many of our high-performing people have left because of the same frustrations? I mean, aside from you.

"I think that in some parts, yes. The difficult thing was that mode of thinking he has; it creates a lot of change of direction. When there are a lot of course corrections coming from the CEO to the leadership team, they sometimes feel they don't have the privilege to go into the details. After a while, your ability to do it paralyzes because they know that there will be another day like this very soon, and it goes on repeat. This is what causes burnout."

Why do you think some of these good ideas and suggestions from critical team members, who were clearly hired for their expertize, have been shut down?

"I think that some of their suggestions for improvements were the optics of optimizing an existing process. Rather, to the CEO, he was looking at a different goal, which is constantly creating new businesses. So, I think it's just a conflict of visions, basically. I mean, that's one part of the problem. The second part that I think is, again, this impact of constant change of directions. It means that the time between a new idea being incepted and digested by the

leadership team or the high performers that can internalize it and create a proper solution is sometimes longer than the time it takes for a new will. So, the slower pace, in my opinion, has led to his frustration and less of others' ideas being implemented."

What's your key takeaway from this experience?

"For me, the key takeaway lesson is that people who want to find their own companies need to be conscious of the velocity of each team, and they need to match their velocity as closely as possible with their collaborators. So, they minimize the amount of frustration that comes from the diversity mismatch, all that they are conscious about. And this mismatching diversity comes to a breakdown of trust, breakdown of patience. In the founder's mind, they need to know that managing all parts of the business (like being a control freak) because he wants things to move at his pace, will end up losing a lot of value because the job of the CEO is to provide a vision and to move forward not to move each individual muscle in the body."

That's a fascinating thought in terms of having a vision is great but being able to build is better. Can we expect founders to let go?

"As an entrepreneur myself, I do understand why it's very difficult to let go. The thing that made you successful once, if you delegate, it feels like you're losing control and you're basically letting go of a recipe for success. I mean, that's mostly what founders provide. But then, at some point, they have to delegate the actual craftsmanship to somebody else. And whether that's team management, Technology Management, Business Development at some point, as the founder you have to let go. So, it is just highlighting how important the recruitment process is but also the onboarding process of your team members. I think during the onboarding period is the time where you can actually

validate that you made the right choices and then make sure that the company culture that you want to have is designated properly."

THERE WAS NO PURPOSE EXCEPT TO "GET IT DONE"

I was told that as the coach, my sole responsibility was to get people engaged; however, with an instant judgment that I had not tried to achieve this. The discussions were short-lived because I would have instantly been directed to do so and failed simultaneously.

While facilitating a workshop for the Product team, I was told I should "Get Them Engaged," and then told that I shouldn't bother trying to do this in the first 10 minutes of my opening mention.

However, I had already had at least two conversations before that point and shared detailed information for my preparation work. On the contrary, what would have been more applicable was if I had approached certain situations and used appreciative inquiry to find out the context from multiple perspectives. It was as if my effectiveness judged people based on previous experiences with other people, i.e., other coaches had left waving their white flags as they exited the business, usually in less than a week.

Our Head of Marketing at the time was in despair as she said, "He (CEO) wants the deck to be created and shared this Wednesday, and then I think he expects it all just to happen. I am not concerned about the timing but more about the challenges in our communication style, demanding behavior, and destructive relationship."

The deck mainly presents a process with our principles and values, so it feels impossible for me to overlook this factor that we don't behave the way we broadcast it. I have experienced this more and more, and it's a culture of urgency when really, we need to be asking what's accurately essential to focus on. I genuinely have experienced and believe that "Slow is Smooth and Smooth is Fast." We just need to get to that realization point.

VERY LITTLE APPRECIATIVE INQUIRY WHEN SOMETHING IS NOT DONE OR FAILS

This tactlessly creates a blame culture, and judgment is applied instantly with the fear of being honest.

There was a situation when the hired coach was initially given a list of tasks and steps of analysis workshop setup. She had completed all but one to a tee and followed a different approach for this last task simply because she had applied her experience to make it a better experience for the team.

While she didn't put the exact steps of how people should be doing the analysis, it was also clear to her that it was not just a good thing but she had already discussed it with the attendees the day before. As the CEO showed up in observation mode that morning, he imprudently called off the workshop and asked that another team leader run it the next day, following his exact instructions this time.

"I had done it because it promotes self-organization this way, which is why I was hired. Instead, I felt like I was instantly judged for not doing this properly, with no questions at all to understand my point of view. If questions had been discussed, I could have shared the many hours of my time spent creating this better workshop as people panicked when the workshop was called in such urgency last night." Ms. Coach defended her actions.

"As a coach as well, I would have appreciated that he had asked questions to create a shared understanding and to allow other points of view to be held. We need to be able to create empathy here. We could start by focusing less on the lists of steps and abstract up to the objective level and finally allow the team to fill that space. I have to admit that he didn't really ask me many questions before he came to me and requested that I create this workshop while telling me exactly what to put in it. Where I have challenged, it then turns into what he wants to see. All he seems to want is a tactical solution, for now. While the team is desperately crying out for a strategic direction to anchor all of their focus. The team's engagement has been very low, and the capability to operate against what is asked is an evident struggle, which if he had asked me about, he would be able to understand the reality better."

THE CONSTANT CHANGE OF DIRECTIONS CREATED CONFUSION, EVEN FOR THE BEST OF US

The employees were lost because nothing was ever enough or good enough. There was no pause to breathe, no time to celebrate, and no opportunity to reflect. The CEO became the organizational saboteur, guilty of burning out its employees without fully realizing that the problem stemmed from these sadly repetitive behaviors.

As the leadership team was on the hook for executing the countless changes that seemed to happen too often now, this team of managers went into exhaustion as they continued to overwork themselves due to the lack of consistent prioritization. The team had lost two weeks just trying to keep pace with the latest change of direction with a new business plan without being given the honor to evaluate the idea before mobilizing their team to action.

For each project or demand, the time, cost (financial or effort), and quality were all non-negotiable, which meant they were likely to be penalized if one of these slipped. With "new" projects frequently popping up from the CEO's desires, the management team not only felt disadvantaged from being side barred in the planning but from a consistent underestimation of how long it takes realistically to get things done. This team was undoubtedly set up for failure.

William[2], one of the senior executives of a tech startup based in London, validated my suspicion that one of the more common reasons employees leave, including his recently departed team, was the constant change of directions that dictated their work.

Let's talk about your current environment. The one thing I can draw is people leaving for a couple of reasons. More prominently, the constant change of direction is incredibly difficult for people to keep up with when they feel like they're going nowhere. What's your view on this?

"I feel that this is a very, very strong reason, as in people not seeing where they're going. I'd like to believe that there is a selection criterion to try and hire people who buy into some kind of a

---

[2]William is an ex-colleague interviewed who remains anonymous.

mission and just don't work for the monthly paycheck. And the company should be clear if they are trying to do more than just making money, like delivering some social good or solving whatever world issue that might be. And also, as individuals, they want to see their careers progress. The frequent changes in direction are normal in a startup especially, but I think the key here is that it's important to see that some level of change is just necessary because never having change in place is not the desired state. This doesn't drive people's motivation. But, when the change is driven internally, and there is apparently no good reason, it becomes insensible and causes the natural churn.

Where it really goes wrong is if there are changes that first of all happen very frequently, and people don't fully understand why that change is in place. What it will result in is first of all the goalpost that people see ahead of them starts getting moved up to a point where it's just unclear. It makes people feel lost. And the second thing is that again, people want to have autonomy, they want to be able to work out their success rather than being told what to do, but for that to happen, they have to know what success looks like. So again, if these goalposts move around all the time and start to disappear after a while, people will start losing sight and think, 'What is success? How can I be autonomous? If I don't know, where am I going?' I get lost if I want to be a great car driver, but I don't know where to get a license. And leaders are supposed to set these directions. If I just start sitting around, this creates an environment where self-starters who can do a lot on their own are either just reduced to very low-level executions because they also can't get ahead without having the context of the knowledge."

Does it mean they've lost sense of the mission if there is no direction? How does this relate?

"My experience is that a company that is really built on a genuine mission, as in, the founders and the leaders believe in that, they can easily stay true to it. When you have to think about how

to adjust the narrative to stay aligned, that's a bad sign. That often means that your mission is sort of a mask, where your ultimate drivers are something different. This company I'm with, we all talk about how to help people and all that. I am very doubtful that there are a lot of people that genuinely are here to do that."

Okay, so we are saying that if a company has to make minor adjustments because of changing conditions but stay true to the mission, it's much clearer to everyone. But, if the goal is to create a business that makes money, then we create a not so lucrative business. Although, of course, it's not black and white like that. People whose primary goal is to turn a profit business could also actively want to help people. It just needs to be emphasized where the focus lies?

"Exactly! The job I had right before this one, there was a mission there. And we never had to dance around that. We never had to really change it except that we expanded our mission to make it a little more inclusive. It created a bigger market segment for us. And that encouraged really high levels of attention."

Agreeing with William seemed to be the most comforting thing to do at that time. While I reflected on why I joined this company, I also paid attention to people who joined us, not the mission itself. Some came in to deliver the numbers, and they didn't care what we did as a company. However, they were happy just being so they could be doing the same job for a big tobacco or fossil fuel company.

But those are the employees who aren't going to be the ones driving the business forward. Incredibly reliable, skilled as they are, this conversation reminded me that there were fewer instances of these people being part of the engine that presses the company to grow and become better. Yet, they are the ones left behind amid this turbulent time of oblivious change.

We now know some founders may bring the best out of their companies; some are still trapped by their ego and cause the worst memories for others. Be wise and stay alert about with whom you choose to work.

CHAPTER 7

The Collectivist versus
The Individualist

Collectivism versus Individualism has been one of the paramount success factors for startups as we know it. Every founder is persistently reminded of who they need to become and how to behave to run a successful business. These are paramount of all the qualities they're expected to have, albeit most have not done this before. So, what is it about these two distinctions that make them a better leader than the other, and what if I found a way to debunk these superficial terms for startups? Just because it's a critical philosophy that you learn in sociology doesn't necessarily mean that it's the recipe for success in a startup, does it?

A RELATIONSHIP-LIKE CULTURE

A collectivistic society manifests from having close, long-term commitments to any members of the group, sometimes whether a family, extended family, or relationships. While collectivists are motivated by group goals and would readily sacrifice their benefit to recognize their team's success, they are also sometimes seen to be too loyal where it overrides most other rules of engagement.

In general, it is said that there are many benefits of having a collectivistic leader in the community. When everyone makes decisions, real success is when the team typically feels responsible for making the right decisions. They would agree that the best way to solve problems is first to understand the tasks that would benefit the team altogether rather than having a single person lead the ideation of the solution first.

In startups particularly, we expect a culture that shows collaboration in creativity, solidifying team ownership. It's essential to create a platform for the team to have equal opportunities. This way, people can voice their ideas and innovate before deriving a final solution. If they were to undertake a new product, they would work together to understand the market problem and develop the desired outcome based on a new frontier for this team.

I recently discussed this with **Kelly Jackson**, long-time HR Leader, and current Chief People Officer of **Luno**, headquartered in the UK. As she described Luno's founders Marcus Swanepoel and Timothy Stranex as good examples of what collectivist leaders should look like, she was adamant that three years ago she would not have joined the company without this top-line tone.

With the CEO's deep passion for the industry and laser focus on driving long-term change, Marcus had tasked Kelly to ensure that the culture always stayed supportive, inclusive, non-hierarchical, and non-status driven. The company is driven by fairness and desires to do right by their people. Attributing this attitude to a probable background upbringing of the CEO, she believed that he would want nothing else than groupthink in the company.

"It starts from the top, and he deeply cares about people and culture, so for a People Officer like me, the CEO was a natural partner; otherwise, it would be a lonely job if there was no dynamic in this relationship. Because he was supportive of what I do and wanted to get to the best outcome, the energy it took to constantly drive the agenda with debate or challenges felt invigorating rather than defeating.

"That's a really important quality because if he didn't show open support toward me, we wouldn't be able to encourage this democracy in the company, which is great because otherwise, we do get into the emperor's new clothes. The founders embody this mentality down to the smallest decisions, so the big thing that goes across the founders is humility. Although I know, not all founders are willing to behave this way."

Nina Mohanty, on the other hand, after having spent over five years in startups around the globe before setting up her own FinTech, **Bloom Money**, attributes her collectivist leadership style to how she was raised in a family with solid southern cultures.

"I was raised with Asian collectivist values. So, everything that I do is about the greater good. And so, when I think about the context that I'm coming from, the cultural context, I was raised to think about everyone else with a certain degree of humility. If I don't take other people's opinions on board when we're making decisions in a room full of other people, I ask myself, why did I invite them then? It just doesn't make sense to me if this is what I look for in a company, why wouldn't I also become one?"

Merita Ramadani, Head of People in **Payhawk**, another Series B FinTech in Europe, gave me insight into why thriving in a supportive, collectivistic culture was the right environment for her. She had just left a toxic culture created by individualist founders that still made her skin crawl when thinking about it as we spoke.

How do you describe collectivist behaviors in your founder, Hristo Borisov?

"Excellent, clear, respectful communication, I will say. They don't have this behavior of putting others down. These collectivist people want to have groupthink and democratize a lot of what they're set to do. Of course, the CEO inevitably has the most power in the room, but at the same time, he's very open to discussion. It's never, 'it's not possible' type of situation with him. If you have an idea and come up with the right arguments, you can convince him of anything, especially if you believe it's the right thing to do for the company. That's the common goal, right? It's democratic."

How do people work in this culture?

"I always describe it as autonomy and freedom. Although I'm not going to lie and say that the CEO is not often immersed and involved in quite a lot of things, why shouldn't he? It is his company, after all. Especially when we're still in this early stage of Series A, we have more to learn and lose if we fail because we're just starting. He may be involved, but there is trust that people hired are doing their jobs, and so far, this feedback isn't micromanaging as we know it. It is simply making sure we are working towards the common goal. One good thing that came out of this is using your autonomy with a guardrail, almost like your moral compass. That way, you know you're always doing the right thing and won't be fearful of losing your job, which is what happens when there's too much freedom, I feel.

"With groupthink, we want to do things together. But it's very different from just being a community because it can also be toxic that way if it doesn't have the right tones. Everyone is very supportive of each other, but our pod's creation made collaboration better. It acts as a platform for us to communicate better and ultimately creates managers that not only ask about your deliverables but naturally ask questions like 'How can I help you? How can I support you?'"

How would someone know what to look for from the outside that this environment suits them?

"I am a big believer in doing due diligence anywhere or with any person you are going to work with. Find out some of the things you can learn from this company, this person, find out if the founders have had a track record of experience, if not at the very least approach people who have worked with them in the past and ask those questions. Talk to current employees no matter how unwilling they are sometimes, but that's a red flag on its own. Think about it; people don't keep quiet about something good. It's usually the opposite. Don't just look at their company LinkedIn page and get excited. That's what I'm trying to say. And for People/HR leaders, knowing exactly the type of founder you will be working with is the key to whether this is going to be a culture you can help shape or completely fall out of place in."

THEN SOCIETY ARGUES THAT THE OPPOSITE OF COLLECTIVISM IS INDIVIDUALISM

This concept isn't precisely wrong if you think about it. Individualism is a philosophy that focuses on the moral worthiness of an individual rather than the group they belong to, so it is believed to have positive influences on the environments the individual is in. Individualistic systems may enable individuals to choose freely, work autonomously, and act with high social mobility. They lean toward choosing who they want to spend their time and effort with. In the end, we also believe that these individuals tend to be happier due to their strong sense of self-efficacy.

Although these behaviors in cultural contexts mean being independent of others while still actively making social relationships, by contrast, to be independent also means decreased well-being if the individual isn't able to balance their self-awareness with a willingness to improve themselves. We would frown upon this when we think of who we want our managers to be, let alone our CEOs. When a company is in its early stage, with minimal resources most of the time, and a maverick founder, we would expect bad practices in the company, thus turning it into a toxic culture. Founders who cannot engage and influence this way will find themselves in a polarized environment founded on an every-man-for-himself norm.

As much as we don't want to admit it, finding a rotten egg in a community of individualistic founders is not at all problematic. But what if we don't know they exist in a company with a brand that over-shadows the founders' true behaviors?

Anisa[1] opened up about her painful experience working for a group of egotistical individualists. The founders didn't care about anyone but their visions.

*"**Dija** was one of a new crop of startups promising to ship groceries to people's doors in a matter of minutes. It started in 2015 before quickly expanding into more than 100 employees within the first month. To put it into context, this was a CEO that wanted nothing more than hiring for growth and had bulldozed every question raised along the way because being challenged wasn't his cup of tea."*

Why didn't it work out with the founders?

"Individualistic founders, to be honest, are people who just care about themselves. It's very simple. What they say goes, goes. I know it's pretty normal in startups because it's their vision, their company, but it was abrupt and toxic to the environment with

---

[1]Anisa was an ex-employee of Dija who remains anonymous.

this CEO. Whatever Alex said to do, there should be absolutely no argument behind it because 'I've done it this way in the past, so it works' or 'I read an article, so this is how it should be done.' To the extent that the other co-founder would be told to stand down because, according to him, it is 'I have more experience, so we'll do it my way.' This (happened) in every meeting, openly, so you can only imagine what the culture was like if not built on ego and fear together."

How did you get into this?

"What I've learned is that there are two sides to this type of founder. Firstly, they're excellent salespeople, which I noticed they use to secure amazing talent. They would sell you the world and tell you this is going to be the biggest rocket ship on the planet. 'Look at our existing VCs and look at how many people are interested in our plans.' Because I had only spent a few years in start-ups, I didn't see a red flag even if it was right in front of me. Instead, I was excited to be part of this hype. I was so excited about the opportunity and in the back of my mind was how lucky I was to be on this ride. The honeymoon period went by quickly. Soon, I started seeing the real culture in terms of how meetings were run. There was regularly just one individual contributor who would speak the entire time, and nobody else had anything to add. This was the CEO; he would be the only person running the show while everyone else nodded their fearful heads while saying, 'yes.' There wasn't any pushback, which was opposite from where I came from."

What is this hype we're talking about?

"Let's be honest; founders usually have a strong presence, right? So, when we went on a recruitment spree, he was present and approached everyone he could find with a great profile. He only wanted to hire the best, so basically, he went all out. He was messaging everyone on LinkedIn, and if you think about it, people

were flattered being spoken to by the founder himself and him selling the dream. When the recruitment drive was done, it felt like we'd created this cult where everyone was so excited to be part of this making the same mistakes as I did, not noticing the red flags at all. People as senior as operating for decades would have skipped the due diligence they should have done during the hiring process. And till this day, I'm thinking about how this person sold us a dream that wasn't even true."

As an individualist, it's expected that their goal was the only thing that mattered. But to dismiss others' ambitions was also not the quality we want in our leaders. How did the employees cope with this?

"Most founders need to have some sort of egoism in them; otherwise, it's very hard for them to be the only person who believes in their dreams, right? So, by standard, they have to have it. Otherwise, it's very hard for them to be successful because they need to sell a dream out of thin air. This is where I would give them credit. But that's where it should stop.

People join our company to realize their dreams, but they also have dreams of their own no matter how small. For example, we proposed different initiatives, and every time he said this is a derailment, it's unimportant. We're talking about critical things like equalizing salary, benchmarking, or creating parental leave policies. Simply put, it's wasn't the main focus because it wasn't his main focus, and that's it; everyone else needed to follow. Most people would be told to focus on recruiting and onboarding people, and for my HR team, nothing else but hiring super-fast was the goal. There was no understanding that while we were growing this fast, little critical things needed to be done in between. 'We don't need an employee handbook,' he once told me. As long as he's superficially comparing us with our competitors, you would be lucky if the job wasn't just recruiting or raising money.

So, to me, this fits perfectly into individualism at its worst because what mattered to him were his own goals. And so, it became extremely painful for me to do this role because my job was to look after everyone else, and I couldn't."

It sounds like the culture suffered from it. How were employees feeling over that time?

"This is where it is interesting. We had two batches of joiners. The first were the ones who followed them, joined as the founding team. These people had worked with them in the past and had somehow gotten over this bruising. They also came from a workplace known for its disreputable culture. Everyone in London would know it.

The second batch, including myself, were people from other places. So, because of the way people weren't allowed to raise questions or stand up for their ideas, it created a culture of fear. Like I mentioned before, my honeymoon period was short. When highly talented people started leaving the company after working closely with the CEO, people got into more fear because leavers would leave without any explanation. We deliberately scaled back our communication to avoid questions. Employees who had just joined would start questioning why their manager had changed after saying yes to the offer two weeks ago. People worried they would be next because there was no reason to fire them. At least not reasons they were allowed to know about. So yeah, it was a bit of a disaster."

Do you feel maybe now you've learned that the person is more important than the brand itself?

"Absolutely, I was too caught up in the hype and forgot to do my research. When I joined, though, they hardly had a brand yet (of course, it's different now), so it would have been much harder to find out the truth unless I worked there. But now, 100 percent like

you say. It's so much easier to get caught up with the brand because of their recent joint venture. They were definitely on track to expand all over the world now. I am fearful for those who don't know this and end up going through burnout as I did. I would want to see where the founders started. What they did in the past, their accomplishments, and I would like to find all of that from people who worked with them before."

THE MISPERCEPTION OF INDIVIDUALISM IS USUALLY A BAD INGREDIENT FOR STARTUPS

Although they're not wrong because it is relatively easy to find a lousy individualist, right? I know what you're thinking now. I must have worked for one and hated it. On the contrary, this was a startup that had done many things it shouldn't have in my perspective, but to this day, having individualists in the culture isn't all bad.

While loyalty is paramount to a collectivist culture, the downside is that individualists often quell their interests. It turns into an unfavorable situation when its adherents prioritize the group because incentives and moral rights all occur on the level of the group, not the level of the individua. This, in turn, makes no room for decisions and accountabilities. On the other hand, individualist operators are very comfortable working with autonomy and sometimes build higher-performing cultures.

At first, I didn't think I could be right, so I reached out to discuss the difference of both with another long-term operator, Fran,[2] who had led people teams in some of the most prominent unicorn startups in Germany.

I reflected on my own experience as she compared them and why one suited her better.

"I worked for two companies, one after the other, and can I just say, I didn't realize how much I did not enjoy the one that

---

[2]Fran is a People expert operating closely with startup founders in Berlin.

everyone is looking for. To put it into context, Company A had collectivist founders who were so heavy on being purpose-driven that they had created a culture that didn't care if they went out of business as long as they were doing something for the planet. Versus Company B where the individualist founder is (a lot) more successful because he was serious about being profitable."

I would have expected the opposite, but I'm not surprised either. What exactly didn't work for you?

"The culture was ultimately the reason I left Company A in the first place. You see, when you're a collectivist leader in an early-stage startup that has a limited budget and resources, often you hire what you can get rather than hire what we call pedigree people who come with experience. So, more so than ever, you end up with this collection of people with great ideas that don't have the capabilities to execute these ideas. Let's put it this way, when your company is bottom-heavy with people who are freshly coming out of school, or they have bounced around in the startup ecosystem, they will come packed with lots of opinions, but there is no real knowledge of having done this before. There's no real foundation from where these ideas are springing. Am I generalizing? Probably yes, but it's common."

Perhaps let's put it this way, maybe it didn't work because this type of collectivism didn't allow for diversity.

"Maybe yes, evidently this was a company that hired their kind, so honestly, I felt out of place most times. We had a collectivist CEO who encouraged us to see everyone's ideas, and when this happened frequently, it manifested in the company. As much as I believe that the best ideas win, this is also not the reason I wanted to join a startup. I wanted to be part of the success. This was, in fact, a 15-year-old company and had only been profitable one year earlier. The business was sustained out of VC money, and they hadn't been able to scale based on achievements;

rather, it was about maintaining this fun playground with resources outside of the company to keep the peace. Of course, people were having fun in a workplace that didn't talk about anything serious.

Coming from established profitable companies to this space, I witnessed how the company's days are numbered simply based on ideas and creativity, not from executing with success. This unbridled democratization led us down a poor path, and I find it manifested more frequently in collective spaces."

So, what you're trying to say is that this company wasn't trying to mature over time, but they had stayed static with little change?

"At one point, it felt like a youth hostel. We became an ideation lab rather than a company because it's all about 'my ideas, my ideas,' and no one was coming up with new products at all. Yet, our employees became entitled because we had created this culture where everyone had a say in everything. There was pressure from wanting the best benefits to staying competitive, but how were we meant to get these things if we weren't making any profits? So, we continued sucking from our investors year on year out. That's where I believe we started to get more complacent because what's the worst that could happen, right?"

I don't think everybody wakes up one day and thinks they're going to create the best company by becoming the best person. But what's evident is that there have been so many failures. We read more about them than successful companies caused by founders' leadership styles. So, for the same reasons, founders are now conditioned by this social acceptance to be the person they're probably not supposed to be. One example is being the nice person in the room while running the business. Otherwise, VCs won't invest, or they can't hire any employees. Does it seem like they can't help it?

"Exactly, I also sometimes blame the VCs because if they were investing and giving these founders resources to build a business, they should get equally involved in observing the way they run the business, not just purely transactional. But the landscape has changed so much in recent years. VCs are now also bombarded to do the right thing, such as investing in a nice person, so really, it turned into a vicious cycle all because it started from a social norm. How would they know if they were standing in front of this mega smart, super nice communal person who is running the business like it's a Playground?"

What about Company B?

"(Companies) run by an individualistic founder, it just recently became the country's newest unicorn. While it's very successful this way, it also has some communal elements that worked for us. The CEO is an individualist because although he had been a successful founder before, this company was his pride. He was determined to ensure it is (moving) in one direction, and over the years, he learned to democratize the way we raise our opinions. At the end of the day, he had a vision and a strong opinion on where to steer the ship. He knows where we need to be. He does entertain ideas, but there is no guarantee that you'll get signed off. So, for me, individualism does not mean caustic."

What about his leadership style made it work?

"He's a caring man. He cares about the employees, and he cares about the business. Whenever I said to him, 'Let's do this initiative,' he was on it. We can see that the ship is steering towards success rather than veering off in every other direction just because somebody decided that they had the 'Montessori hour' and came up with an idea. Things that can be embedded in the strategy came from long thought processes. Whenever he didn't initially agree with an idea, he would bend towards his better judgment to be inclusive and hear them out. So, this wasn't

a hippie commune like Company A because the issue with over-grown communities is that we forget we're a business and we're supposed to be profitable at one point.

Over here, it's clear to everyone that our CEO needed us to help him get there, and you will be rewarded for your hard work because it's simple logic for us. You should get your salary increases because the company is doing well, so much so from a people leader perspective; I want to give them everything, but they've got to give something back, right?

As an employee, my experience in this individualistic environment is ironically also one of the more successful startups I've worked in thus far. If I were a more junior employee, I would enjoy this communal thing instead because it would be built on my ego. I get to go to work and see myself in all hands. As a senior person, however, the important things to me are in contrast to that. Clear communication in terms of okay, what's the plan? Are we hitting the targets? Are we on course, and are the right people in the right place to get us there? While I don't need to jump around on stage and all hands because we've hired 100 employees and have a superficial celebration about it, it's more comforting for me to know that the company I'm working for is in great shape so that I can get a salary increase and get my bonus. Maybe I don't see myself in every single project, and that's okay."

As far as I'm concerned, what you're describing in this communal environment is similar to communism, maybe just a different version of it. How do you make sure the culture is honest about it?

"Don't get me wrong when I articulate success in my people's strategies, I create space for people's voices. There is a space for ideation. But this wild people-pleasing where everybody gets a say is the main detractor of success. For example, we were honest about who we are by clearly saying we are a high-performing

company and success-driven. And if you are not all about that, then it is not the right environment for you. I think that more startups would be more successful if they kind of just called it and were more honest."

Would this culture of performance work for everyone, though?

"For the year and a half that I was there, I only took one day off, and it wasn't burnout as I would describe it. It was a high-performing strategy that was mainly exhilarating. On the other hand, a heavily communal environment burned me out instead. Let me tell you how it happened. When you are in this kind of laissez-faire culture where everyone is sitting around without even trying, you very quickly become the enemy of the state.

Simply put, I was performance-driven, and the others were not. So, what you see is them playing ping pong while I'm working extra hours at home because I was still laser-focused on the task. The other problem is that you don't get a lot of support when you're in this environment. You want to believe in the essence of a community because most times, people are there for you without actually doing the work. So, they're not helping to be honest. So, to me, this was much more dysfunctional than those high-performing environments because you're such an alien. What I learned from this experience was that they should have never hired me in the first place.

The CEO or the founders are the ones who set the tone from the top in their ivory tower. If they have created this laissez-faire culture, they've created entitlement in the employees. People leaders then get asked the big question, 'Why are my employees feeling entitled?' Well, that's because you haven't been punishing them for not delivering. And you haven't rewarded them for the same reasons, which effectively means you're not being fair. And even more than that, I think you almost punish hard-working people because they pick up the slack, right?

This is where an individualist shines through as a leader with their ability to stay focused. If there was no need to be individualistic, we could have a communal atmosphere. If I trusted that they all have the same desire and energy, they have the same drive to make something happen. Then the CEO would have allowed us to do whatever as long as we got to the right result, which mirrored his vision for the company. That would be an ideal state."

As I listened attentively to what Fran described as the better experience working for an individualistic leader, I couldn't help but reflect on one of my better memories working at Revolut. While this was a culture where everyone was there for their own goals, it was also evident that we wouldn't have been able to achieve our goals if it wasn't overshadowed by the founder's objective ultimately.

Everything we did was tasked directly by the CEO himself, and it only served one purpose: to build a successful business. Since I've left the company years later and mostly found myself in communal environments, I realized right about the two-year mark that it did not fit my identity or personality. Because I realized I wasn't being true to myself. Instead, I was trying to fit in, which meant the effectiveness of my work wasn't top quality as more performance-driven colleagues would have surrounded it.

For several years after leaving the company, there was also a social thing where I would feel unaccepted if I behaved a certain individualistic way simply because there was so much stigma around it. It comes with a definition of not caring about your people or that you're not being human enough. It also meant you might not have empathy to lead if you are just very laser-focused on succeeding.

Although most people looked at me with sympathy whenever they asked me to relive my experience working there, the truth is it didn't work out because I wasn't able to forge a better relationship with the CEO. A closer relationship would've led to a more beneficial outcome.

Instead of the tarnished culture, I vividly recalled how it was one of the most exciting experiences I've had working alongside some of the most intelligent people I've met. The right culture can give employees what they want to get out of this experience. Suppose the downside of creating communities is the lack of accountability amongst people who hide behind each other and hold hands to solve a problem. In that case, I'd personally prefer the former. With no responsibility, you often end up with no decision-makers because there's absolutely no ownership in people.

So, how can we know who creates the best work environment? Collectivists or individualists?

DE-IDEALIZING COLLECTIVISM

Based on our usual understanding of collectivism, we expect these people to be warm and caring. We want them to be helpful, cooperative, and even feel close to their friends and family. There should be a great deal of trust and mutual support. If networks of obligations do not constrain the environment to community relationships, their individual's true intentions would likely align with their formal commitments at work.

While we might think we want to opt for a workplace culture like this, sometimes that collectivist tendency may not entail trust. It's not crazy to think that this tension exists because of collectivism, not despite collectivism. The tight social ties of this behavior could create community ostracism even with solid communal support.

Take an eager co-worker who offered to help you. They suggest looking over an important project and then going above and beyond to complete the task for you. Some people in this environment would worry that the co-worker would be up to no good. Should anything happen to this project, they might think that this helpful person may be why they won't be successful or promoted next.

This is my perception of the nuances of collectivism, where cultural values and goals are not static and sometimes even exist on a much broader spectrum than we expected. On top of the shifts in cultural standpoints caused by expansion or globalization influences, individualists can be more valuable than collectivists, whether their ideals are inherent or imported, especially in a leader with high construal in these personality differences.

Can we agree that we can have a community of individualists? That's it. You have brought all the individualists together. When you have a weak collectivist CEO, let them group their communal people, and they can go on to take their ship and sail to the middle instead of going into some other company and trying to infect it. The only protection from that kind of mindset is to ensure we're recruiting appropriately. This way, we can see that the aspirations to drive change align with the people you've brought in to do exactly that. As Fran said before we wrapped up our discussion, *"I have a personal perspective that this communal type of culture is designed to shoot for the middle where the individualists shoot for the stars."*

The one piece of advice I would leave you with is that most employees would probably have to experience both environments before knowing what fits them better. Let's look at the employees universally here. I would hope that anyone drawing from my learnings would give them enough insight to say, let me ask better questions about the captain of this ship than the culture. I'd ask them to investigate what it is like to be working there. Better so, ask direct questions about the punishment if they don't hit targets because, let me tell you, if the interviewer can't tell you that there is a punishment and just rewards, then it's probably a laissez-faire culture that isn't taking you to the stars.

What is on the outside may seem different from what is happening inside. Instead of going in blind, if you find yourself in an individualistic culture, perhaps it is time to ask an honest question. Can we aim to build a community of humanistic individualists?

If this vision is correct, it suggests that the answer to cultural psychology's open secret lies more in asking the right questions than in throwing out self-experiences.

CHAPTER 8

The Community Builder

When a startup outgrows itself from its founding location, they spurt into expansion activities to spread their progeny elsewhere in the hope of solving more of the world's problems than they initially set out to. And to do this, most startups harness the communities they have created both internally and externally.

WHAT IS COMMUNITY?

Depending on the context and the company, communities are ultimately a group of people who have come together under a shared purpose. This either refers to the company's mission or, very simply, the product they have created together. But whatever that is, these are people who have intentionally stayed together to communicate, learn, and share.

In recent years, "community" has turned into one of those buzzwords that proudly hailed from Silicon Valley as we saw more swift growth startups talk about their magic to success. We've since seen more startups around the world adopting this method as their core marketing tool, but People leaders (including HR) were beginning to use them to create culture frameworks. Its loyal advocates call it "fundamental in entrepreneurship and culture-building." This is because while most entrepreneurs tend to focus on themselves as the key to startup success, most have connected the reality to the reliance of their community, be it their customers or their employees.

As I work with entrepreneurs in my coaching time, I often see their frustrations from building a startup in the wrong place or wrong time, including insisting that their failures are attributed to personal limitations such as experience, skill, and investment capital. Rarely have they thought about this limitation was caused by their ignorance of new ways to start a conversation as they struggle to put away these so-called playbooks. They forget to connect to the communities around them in this ecosystem they are part of. Let's put it this way; it may not seem fair that, albeit having the perfect product, their company is not where they want it to be, but passion and commitment are not enough to take it further. Every business needs its critical resources. One of them is the connection they have with others.

In *The Startup Community Way* by Brad Feld and Ian Hathaway, they mentioned that while most founders are convinced it's all about having investors, it should have been obvious that critical resources in a startup go far beyond just money. Both writers have over 30 years of experience with Techstars.

The funny thing is communities have been a core part of this conversation since running businesses began. Let's consider some of the more prominent names in the startup world, such as **Clubhouse**. When Clubhouse started, the founders built a community-first approach and kept it in a close network predominantly used to leverage a community of Founders and Venture Capitalists. It helped them become an essential part of the tech conversation that quickly grew and subsequently created a platform for influencers to launch the brand further than it could imagine. They had the right audience, in the right community.

The same goes for **Stack Overflow**, where every day, there are thousands of developers working together to solve problems and pass on these learnings to each other. Started by Jeff Atwood and Joel Spolsky in 2008, it has now become one of the most significant communities for developers, both experienced and aspiring.

The legendary Q&A website for programmers (including Quora) enables the easy availability of programming expertize online. At the same time, other platforms such as GitHub, BitBucket, or Source Forge allow the sharing and re-use of codes, which has dramatically changed how individuals seek help and support from their programming peers. As it expanded, the birth of this community developed, and it became the norm to seek help online, whereas we once relied on a textbook or an office colleague.

While there are success stories from the big names, it doesn't only apply to companies with a large following. Small startups and creators are also beginning to leverage their communities. We start to see brands being conceived out of YouTube, Instagram, and TikTok, such as Expert Coach, Gillian Perkins, and Entrepreneur, Carrie Green. It allows entrepreneurs to present themselves in various unique ways via these platforms. As people now prefer good, fast content such as short videos, they have become one of the most prominent marketing tools today.

Following that, we're beginning to see the importance of communities integrated into hiring plans, expansion strategies, and marketing campaigns. Startups are hiring more community builders and architects as early as possible in their growth. They realize the company's most essential needs are people, internally and externally. They need people who care about their mission and believe in their product while still in startup diapers.

THE ANATOMY OF A COMMUNITY

Communities come in many shapes and forms, including physical or digital forums. However, they share similar anatomy to make it work.

At the heart of every community lies its influencer, sometimes more than a single individual. These are those who drive the community's conversations and shape the way we interact with it. Engagers are the members who, while in a small size, may not influence the direction of the community. They can easily overrule the influencer if they come with opposing views, especially in a large enough size. Striking a delicate balance here is why we see guidelines set on influencers to keep the relationship with their members harmonious, sometimes in a controlled environment—for example, forums with no voting abilities. Finally, we have the followers who are seen as less active and less opinionated than the members. Generally, they are happy to go along with the community in whichever direction they are going, as they are unlikely to feel passionate enough to influence the discussion.

In the make-up of every community, the power of influence isn't limited to their social presence and products, but people. Suppose a startup can't engage its early adopters (customers and employees included) and plant their seeds for a community. In that case, the company cannot develop a movement on its mission which is key to their successes in growth. Therefore, as we dissect the ways communities are built in startups, we also acknowledge that great company cultures, when separated by geo locations, rely on their communities that mainly thrives on all parties, being their employees. Where you see a close-knit startup team, you will also see how collaborative they are as they build a strong foundation of emotional bonds with each other. Often, these employees describe their culture as "caring, transparent, teamwork...and of course, fun." After all, when you appreciate working with your colleagues, it should also be fun.

So, you've started a new business with a new idea. How do you get people to care?

ONE—A COMMUNITY WITH A MISSION

Sometimes, we call this the "feel good" company. Feel-good factors are used in startups that set out to either make you feel good about yourself or have a sense of mission around them as you join their journey. It boosts the endorphins responsible for your mood balance. Simply put, these are companies that help people feel optimistic about the future as they associate with their brand or product.

Some have also been successful purely based on their ability to capture and engage their followers, finally converting them into direct users (customers). Take **Bumble**, for example, a winning startup through adversity. Although we could attribute its success via a series of problems it was solving for our dating lives, Bumble also created a massive following from believing this is the new way of making dating safer for women who found **Tinder** risky. It was a product wholly focused on executing its mission from day one. Bumble steadily gained market share over the seven years and made its way across the world when the app centered entirely around dating for women. From what they're looking for to what makes them comfortable, the exponential growth was due to its ability to amass a huge following as an app created by women for women.

Voi, another up and rising micro-mobility startup in Sweden, vowed to bring a better solution to the scooter-riding community in a region with one of the highest percentages of users compared to the rest of the world ensuring their customers understood why this was important to them. As it turns to AI to enable its scooters to detect pedestrians and sidewalks, it announces its mission to allay riders and the cities' safety fears.

Community is the center of how Voi has expanded its market reach over the last three years since it launched. As the pandemic hit front-line workers who couldn't afford to stop working, the startup offered free rides to hospitals across the Nordics and increased the placements of their scooters closer to healthcare sites.

They were also recently working closely with the visually impaired community to build more diverse products that will break barriers to their service provision and develop our communities proactively. Speaking to James,[1] their People Operations manager, about the company's main reasons in keeping close to their ecosystem, it was clear to him that the external views were not far from its internal culture. The company is tightly bound by its ability to share information and experiences. It was the main reason he committed to its goals over the last 12 months. According to James, the CEO Fredrik is strong on making it their mission to treat its employees the way they treat their customers, *"After all, we're also our own customers."*

Another Unicorn startup that is now taking the HRTech world by storm is **Personio**, one that has also recently created a new market category to bring solutions to solve a full suite of complex employee management problems from compensation to productivity. But we ordinary people don't know Personio for its game-changing products but the presence of their community. As I discussed the ins and outs of going through daily life in the company, **Sam Richards**, their Country Manager of UK, explained that it has always been a top-down approach.

Did you mean the founder pushed for communities to be created?

"I think most tech startups now try to build a community from the beginning as it is now broadly acknowledged how having a strong culture and community can positively impact a business. And I think it is always going to have longevity and survive, and thrive in fact, as it faces the constant change and growth that startups typically face, if it is authentic and seeded by the founders.

[1]James is a current employee of Voi, based in Sweden who remains anonymous.

"When I first started at Personio, I asked Hanno, our CEO, how he was thinking about the culture and sense of community at Personio as the business had grown so rapidly both in terms of successes and headcount. At nearly 1,000 employees, he explained how much of a bedrock the culture and community are and so is continually pinning every decision back to the company values and operating principles. So yes, it comes from the top."

At what point did you think we as a society decided this was a good, if not better, way of working?

"My perception is it is probably somewhat connected to a new generation of leaders and workforce that have had a different experience growing up to previous generations; with more access to information, and more understanding for how much more fulfilling spending time in a community of people passionate about working together toward a common goal could be.

It looks alien now to watch movies made only 30 years ago where the characters would go to work, sit in a cubicle watching the clock, and then go home again. For this generation, and particularly in startup tech you want a work-life blend, where you get joy out of every working day.

As an employee, I think it does two things: It is beneficial in motivating you to do more for the business because if that didn't exist, it takes away that drive to move forward and do better together. Secondly, people are more thoughtful in a community—willingness to share best practices, broaden your network, ask people for help when you need it, and together share when things are bad or good.

I think it makes you feel more included quickly. Join any business without that sense of community and it can take a long time to integrate because effectively, you are kind of waiting for your window to be invited in. And that it's essential because even if you're an extrovert, everybody wants to be wanted; everybody wants to be invited to the party. Without a strong culture to support it, that community that might be there in early days organically, can easily divide as the company scales.

Think about it, right, you've got the old school people who've been here a long time, and then you've got the new wave, plus if you're split by geography, the more organically divided you get. So, I think having that sense of community helps speed up your integration and drives more engagement from my perspective."

Speaking of integration, scaling too fast might break the good thing you have going on. How can we avoid it?

"Recruiting the right way is key here. Does it work for everyone? Probably not. But I will say that this working style is very appealing to millennials. But suppose you are honest in your hiring cycle. In that case, you will effectively attract enough diversity of thought while consistently bringing in people who will continue to build that community and want to be community builders. You can't be somebody who joins that kind of business if you don't like it because it would be an awful place to work. That's the top line the way I see it."

Who's responsible for it? I mean, we hear people say, "It's the CEO's job to do that." Is it, though?

"I think top-down is the most sensible but not making the CEO the single point of failure here. Buy in is incredibly important, but there needs to be an ethos driven from the top and then filtered down so that the responsibility doesn't necessarily sit with the top to go consistently. But he has to set the tone. I have a memory of a company that didn't have this sense of community. Building that sense of community bottom-up was challenging because reality is like anything. If you don't have executive buy-in, it's very challenging to make it a consistent and authentic environment that is a natural way of working.

"Otherwise, you may have it in silos and teams, but does it come across that same way in everything? No. We had specific initiatives and wanted to set our OKRs in a reflective element, but it was easy to spot the disparity. Simply put, if you had two or three people who were not bought into that and didn't live it, it would start to dilute the pool. It takes a lot of investment to ensure that the community continues to thrive and is the foundation of business."

What about external factors detracting it from the focus through evolution?

"In the earliest stages, you will have investors, but they will sit separately from the business. The closer you move toward your financial event, whether an exit or an IPO, these investors' needs become much more apparent. Therefore, that will become a more significant guiding point for how the business has to perform. And at this point, I think companies have an exciting decision to make from the top: you have additional pressures that you maybe did not have before. You see many Series A Series B having fun because they have loads of money and can do all these things, launch events, and have company trips because you still have the time and energy to invest in the things we believe in. But as time goes on and investor pressure becomes more, you might lose sight of that. There's no secret that balancing it is critical because suddenly, your audience has changed. The shareholders are not necessarily community builders."

TWO—A WHOLE COMMUNITY AROUND THE FOUNDER/S

Greg Isenberg (Founder, Investors, Tech Influencer) tweeted once on the common misperception between building an audience versus a community as most companies misunderstood their value. According to Isenberg, companies who get this wrong tend to focus on a single individual rather than building a community that focuses on people who can participate and contribute to the same conversation. This is when the influencer and the member are the same person.

It can be good, like how Steve Jobs is Apple. But it can also be bad because Apple had a cult culture. NYU professor Erica Robles-Anderson, a cultural historian, once mentioned in 2015 as she examined the brand and declared, "It's a cult. Right? It's so obviously a cult." It is a brand that creates hype around its release days by pushing for inclusivity. You would feel left out if you weren't part of the wait.

This seemed to be the case for **Revolut**, a giant FinTech in the UK that built a community externally stronger than its internal. Did it matter that the company is known for its tarnished toxic culture? Not really, no. Sure, they might have lost some customers, but they were never short of customers with a product as versatile as theirs. Countless followers would ignore the notoriety of their infamous culture and remain loyal in the conversation from day one. Because of how the brand was derived from having a "genius" founder, they continue to get out of jail free passes as the mass majority encourages his destructive behaviors. Equally, enough of them hate the optics and avoid being their customer because of one person's influence, the Founder.

According to **Marisa Bryan**, Talent Acquisition Leader, who was appalled by the experience of Revolut's (and a few more) hiring process, had a lot to say about the aftertaste it left on her as their customer (ex). And Revolut wasn't the only one that made her no-go list.

"People are just who they are. Think about it. If you're working somewhere where everybody is genuinely good people, you don't end up investing so much of your energy and brainpower trying to fit in and be productive. It's the same when I look up a brand or not. For me, it's the model of all founders or leaders. If you can't be humble and lead with compassion and humility, then you end up losing the staff hand over fist. The famous stories about making people sign new contracts in the middle of the pandemic then making them all redundant after so that they didn't have to pay out the notice periods, that kind of stuff weighs your brand. It adds weight to your customer experience as well. It may be extreme to say this, but I would rather be barefoot than buying something from Sports Direct. Or I'd rather starve than shop in Walmart because you know how they treat their employees.

"For example, when you work at Apple, one of the things that you're intensely aware of is the consumer brand. And the fact that you are, in some cases, the only person that anyone will ever meet who works at Apple. So, we all know the products we are using every day. When I was interviewing people there, they'd say, "Now, what's the point of having the home button?" I need to be able to represent and answer. We're acutely aware that you are the face of a brand that's very well-known, and people will associate you with that. As a result of my experience at Revolut, I canceled my account. I will never use that product. And if anyone had asked me, I would heartily recommend they go with a competitor.

"When I interviewed the CEO of another startup in the UK, **CityM**,[2] I recalled deleting the app from my phone right after that and have never used it again. I think people's experiences as candidates get passed on the same as if you go to a bad restaurant or a lousy coffee shop. It does have an impact on your product. So, to say we're a product-like business, all we care about is the product is a big mistake. We still have to care about the people that you interact with because they're ultimately the ones who want to buy it or use it."

#Girlboss companies, what about them? These are feminist branded companies that became synonymous with the growing demand for being socially responsible. Nine out of 10 Gen Z consumers presently believe that brands have a responsibility to communicate their beliefs, which created a generational demand for female leadership and empowerment to be seen in companies. When we look at the communities they have built around figurehead founders, some of us wonder if it was the clothing that made **Nasty Gal** successful or Sophia Amoruso and what she represented. Did we care about the inventory they sold, or did we want to be part of the conversation? I think the weight falls onto the latter. Simply look at how Nasty Gal went bankrupt in 2016 amid claims of toxic workplace culture and especially the publicly known allegations of the company firing employees for being pregnant.

---

[2]London-based startup.

Over time, it has become a must for startups to derive their brand via their communities constructively. When a community culture comes directly from the founders, it could go either way, as we have seen at Revolut, CityM, or Nasty Gal. But what if it stems from communally sensible founders?

Here in Europe, **Pleo** (a Danish Tech Startup) has a mission to help businesses rethink how to enable their employees to buy the things they need for work while keeping it centralized for control. Set up in 2015 by FinTech Veterans, Jeppe Rindom and Niccolo Perra, Pleo started building a community within its ecosystem from day one quickly before being known as one of the best places to work on LinkedIn's Top 10 Startup list in 2020. Many had expected it to be a successful startup even before it finally reached Unicorn status earlier this year. Their Community and Marketing Manager, **Victoria Murphy**, attributes their ongoing triumph to their strong community-based culture.

What were the early days like at Pleo?

"When I joined Pleo, we were still in our scrappy, early stage figuring it all out, but even when we closed Series B, people were just starting to know who we were. We realized we didn't necessarily have brand awareness out there. So, we thought to ourselves, how do we relate to people out there?"

How do you keep it steady while growing so fast?

"A lot of it has to do with the people we hired from the start because lots of people buy into the mission and the values behind the products and, of course, behind the leaders. We believe in Jeppe and Nicco, and even now we're a Unicorn, we still get people that are more driven by success than anything else like, 'no, this is going somewhere, and I want to be on this ride.' Somehow, along the way, we created this type of community culture and we just kind of amplified it externally because it's what we know best.

I would say that at Pleo, that all comes from the C-level team, if not directly from the founders. So again, it is groupthink. It's clear to us. We have two co-founders in how we communicate or work because they practice what they preach. Even as we grew bigger like we are now, we still tried to take parts of the good. For example, in the earlier stages, Jeppe would bring people into the board meetings, so they understood what was going on. And then try to have them shadow him just for transparency. We can't do that with 400 people, but instead, we switched it up. We show employees our performances, and they'd still be honest whenever it got difficult for us. They could have hidden away and just been focusing on the numbers, but instead, they were like, 'This is okay, we've got this.' And I think that speaks volumes."

Why do you think a culture of togetherness is so influential?

"In a startup, often you have founders who are these unnamed, silent figures in the distance that you can't access. If that person is like the brains behind the product, or they're a fantastic businessperson but not a people person, then it will not go very far. As leaders, if you don't win their hearts and minds, you lose that goal at the end of the day. When I see our leadership team, they are a complementary group. Everyone understood their gaps, but there was a desire to be better. It's not always the case in startups."

When I look at Pleo, there's a real sense of community that embraces both the external and the internal. Tell me about the reason behind it.

"I think people can tell when a company is lying. So, you can say you're transparent or say that we all care about each other and we're super flexible. People will find that very quickly because there are things like Glassdoor or LinkedIn and even just word-of-mouth. And I think the startup circle is small enough for you to find out if that wasn't the case. So, I think from an early, early moment on, we put relationships in the center of what we do. When we care and cater to our employees, it lends itself to how we are perceived externally. So now we get the talent, and now we get the customers.

Because of the way we behave, other people gravitate towards that. The community helped us out, got us businesses, recommended us to others, and it just became who we are and what we want to be known for. We say this a lot: 'You scratch my back. I'll scratch yours.' So, I think it's a case of building these partnerships and building these brand friendships."

How do you think the company can stay true to this long term? I mean, at some point, directions or priorities might change.

"It's an honest and humble culture internally. We get told all the time how fantastic we are, which is brilliant, but we're also acutely aware of all the things we're not fantastic at. So, we keep evolving. Because I think deep down, I believe that the present won't sustain us if we don't keep moving forward. And I'd say honesty helps because you can just be yourself at Pleo, which is good, and how much you give of yourself is down to you. Some people share their big personalities, and some people are a little bit more laid back or reserved, and that's fine, too."

What would it be like, do you think, if they were different founders?

"I genuinely can't think of better founders that I worked for or I've heard of anyone working for. So, I think because they've been so involved from day one and if they were suddenly not to be there I think things would be very different. I don't know who would like that place. They're the kind of people who know 150 people's names off the bat.

I don't personally see how anyone else is going to be able to come in and do that. And that's just the way they've cultivated Pleo because they genuinely care about the people they bring on, as well as the product. So yeah, I think if they were to go, I think a lot of people would follow, and then if they were to set something new up, I think a lot of people would then say, 'I want a piece of that because I know exactly the kind of magic that they bring when they're together."'

THREE—A TRAGICALLY MISALIGNED COMMUNITY

What if the startup doesn't necessarily have a mission to build a safe place for its employees but is only more prosperous thanks to its strong bond with its community?

"Move over marketing. If your product has a community culture, you will find that word-of-mouth is all you need," said my colleague, Marketing Director one morning as we were celebrating hitting 10,000 signups in our waitlist for something that hadn't even been launched yet.

HOLD ON, WHAT IF THERE WAS A FOUNDER WHO DIDN'T DO WHAT HE PREACHED?

On the contrary, a startup can still disillusion its community (and employees) when they fail to align their mission to actions. A **UK Health Tech Startup, Babylon Health** set out to make high-quality healthcare accessible and affordable for everyone. It went on a journey to achieve this and most recently IPO-ed the company making it one of the top up-and-coming companies in the European market to date. The startup surely tried to show a sense of care towards its ecosystem by being a digital-first health service provider that uses an artificial intelligence-powered platform to bring virtual appointments to everyone in the easiest form of access. This is a company that we had hoped would eventually give every person in the UK the ability to see a GP (General Practitioner). Due to its convenience, it has been called out to cherry-pick low maintenance patients rather than those who might require more treatment. In 2019, *Wired* journalists also called out the company's safety-first culture that was anything but "right" at all times.

Despite this, they still have plenty of followers. While the company doesn't disclose their user numbers, it has been discussed to be over

100,000 after a quick check on their app downloads in the Apple store. So why does their Glassdoor page scream out the following reviews?

*"**Bad decisions, poor management.**"*

*"**Horrible working experience here.**"*

*"**Management is supposed to empower you, not lord over you or treat you badly.**"*

*"**For a healthcare company, little to no focus on mental health. If asked for it, you'll be laughed out the door.**"*

And these are just a few.

My first thought was how all of the external glamor does not match how employees were treated. According to one of their recent leavers, Georgia,[3] an HR Manager who tendered her resignation as soon as her stock options were fully vested. "Not a minute more..." was how she started our discussion over the disenchantment of working there the last three years.

So, Georgia, tell me about this irony.

"Simple, (he) just wasn't invested in people or us all together. While he was trying to do something amazing for everybody by putting healthcare in the hands of everybody, he didn't care about people, at least not those around him. I mean, his wife was our COO, and even she was shouted at openly in front of the company. I didn't struggle with him because I was brought in to solve problems. But did he care about me? Absolutely not. There was no investment in the culture piece. He didn't care even with the engagement data we presented to him. He just didn't want to talk about us. Period."

---

[3]Georgia was an ex-employee of a UK-based healthtech startup.

I don't understand. The brand talks about creating this socially supporting community, but was there nothing of this sort?

"It's a very weird one. When anyone was invested in culture, it was from our chief of staff. When she left, the conversation just went out the window. Anyone who wanted to 'save the people' was basically pushed out because it just wasn't important."

But the company continued to perform?

"This is why it's so hard for me to fathom as well, and I'm in the People team where I see it all. Aside from all of that, the company was still doing amazing because I was the one that was asked to hire, create contracts, or bring on new clients everywhere. But that wasn't communicated then with the wider business. There was a lot of ambiguity around the company."

Did it not matter, though? The perception, reputation, and how it would affect business altogether?

"It didn't because we were selling it to more prominent companies, and not all clients asked how our people were feeling, right? It's a misperception. So many similar founders out there with Unicorns, so why would we be any different? Honestly, it was like an 'almost Titanic.' A sinking ship that just hasn't happened yet."

FOUR—A COMMUNITY THAT EXTENDS A CONVERSATION

Not all startups will be the next Apple, but they all have one thing in common, to solve a common problem. Communities born out of startups like this often create new conversations either socially or around the solution they have brought into the world. Some even create new categories, pioneering areas that haven't yet been explored.

On the other hand, **Karma** or **Too Good To Go** are startups that offer a marketplace to let local restaurants and groceries offer unsold food at a discount, fighting against food wastes in the world.

While these companies may not have yet been noted on the success map, they have certainly started a discussion on how much food waste we contribute to our planet daily. Understanding the implications of it had created a social movement we needed.

This community provides a venue to share ideas, exchange advice, collaborate, and, more importantly, celebrate together. **Cadran Cowansage,** the CEO/Founder of **ELPHA**, created an open group for women to find support in the startup space. Launched out of Y-Combinator in 2019, the best thing you'll find on the platform is that amazing women support each other and build a strong women's culture.

On the other hand, entrepreneur and **Professor Teresa Tamayo, Ph.D.,** set up the Women in Tech community on the other side of the world, basing it in Spain. As a non-profit organization giving visibility and boosting the women startup ecosystem worldwide, she described the reasons behind **W Startup Community** in 2015 as a necessary way to extend the conversations about breaking down barriers for women to enter the tech profession.

The same goes for **Marissa Ellis**, who, after 20 years of working in corporate tech, decided to build a company that continues bringing us closer to a diverse and inclusive workforce this industry desperately needs. Running **Diversity** is more than just fulfilling her entrepreneurship goals. Its objective is to build an incredibly supportive and empowering community of activists, advocates, and allies who want to support each other. Her team's work when they go into organizations is about trying to get that kind of energy and enthusiasm into the mindsets of everyone. Through their inclusive leadership training, they are teaching leaders about the key things that should be embedded into the way they think and their decisions. Even just a startup, they aimed to change one mind at a time.

She positively confirmed that the community has grown year by year and attributed its success to being able to build on awareness more than anything.

"I think, in essence, it's creating awareness more than anything. I've spent a good couple of decades in the tech industry, and for probably two-, three-quarters of that, there were so many things that I didn't challenge. It wasn't that I was scared to challenge, but I had the same blind spots. You know, I thought it was okay for me to be the only woman in the room. I didn't think that was a massive problem if we were all doing a good job. I didn't know how wrong I was because there wasn't. This lack of diversity conversation meant that we were blinded by our lack of knowledge and our lack of awareness.

"So, building this company centered around that sense of mission has honestly made this one of the easiest things I have done, plus it is incredibly rewarding to my employees, not just for me."

While some startups are built upon serving a more extensive social purpose, we must not discount those continuing an old-time discussion and bringing it back to the table, such as the new world of HR. Human Resources has been around for as long as any business can remember. Still, the congestion of startups has forced us to realize that there are opportunities to make this a more integral part of building a successful company. **Anouk Agussol**, Founder of **Unleashed**, a consultancy that supports high-growth startups and scaleups through people, culture, and leadership, answered some questions.

Let's talk about Unleashed's great work in creating this new conversation, almost this new way of rethinking HR. Why was this important to the company?

"It's important to me because I think as individuals, every single one of us has the power to influence our little bit of society for the better. There are so many startups and businesses that are small now but are the world's future. And so, I want to be able to work with companies who want to create a better working world, not just a better world. For the employees within the business, for the products, and while they're creating products to disrupt the industry, why can't we also disrupt this old perception of good culture?"

As a consequence of that, you'd hope that this conversation, plus the work you're doing with startups, can then help founders act on this change.

"I think for that to happen well, we need founders who are in the right mindset—those who want to make things better and be the change we want to see. Aside from the typical founders who just want to make a lot of money, we want to help those who want to create a workplace that has fulfilled individuals and impacts society on a bigger scale.

It's important for us to change the conversation and make culture and people in businesses the heart of their business strategy because we think its impact can be far-reaching beyond this state that we're currently in. Because founders come to us, they recognize that they want to get this right, and it's hard to get it right. This means there's already a bias in terms of positive-leaning founders. So, does having a community help? Absolutely, because we have far more aspiring founders reaching out for support than ever now."

STARTUPS RELY ON THEIR COMMUNITIES FOR SUCCESS

It's been evident that the importance of community is at an all-time high as we see more startups show a solid intent to build large, engaged, and loyal communities around their brand. But what is a community? So far, we've seen a generalisation that communities are people who like each other or at least being around each other. But on the contrary, some may argue that just because you are friends or being friendly or simply enjoying conversations doesn't mean you can work together. The fact that there are so many disparities between different cultures in different companies shows that individuals depend on more profound learning.

Let's simply put it this way. Maybe you are a first-time founder, or perhaps you have done this several times. It is not guaranteed that you are the expert to scale every time. And as your growth depends on your people and your people depend on your culture, you have the opportunity to rely on your internal and external "friends" to help you maintain this success along the way. And this is the value your community brings to the table. On the other hand, those companies have trouble managing this part of growth. They lose track of what's essential at this stage when they focus on hyping their communities the wrong way, i.e., running events that bring no revenue or having a pizza night with the team but still expecting them to come to work the following day at 9:00 a.m. Founders need to understand that culture isn't something written down somewhere to get their people to swoon over it. It's about bringing real value to each other, such as common grounds and passion. After all, a community is created to provide support and solve problems together, right?

So, what next? Now that you've got your community rolling, it's important to keep it growing by steadily bringing in more people to keep the energy high. Keep bringing in people gradually. Be patient. Before you know it, you'll have a large, thriving community that will serve as the foundation of your company, product, and customer base for years to come. The best thing for us to do is let the ecosystem take its place in evolving our cultures as we adapt to the changes, but what if the founders decide that their personalities and preferences come first? We'll explore cultures birthed under these conditions in Chapter 9.

The Keen Learner

Essential for learning in startups, we know that all founders aspire to be something they see as a measure of their version of success. That's why it is difficult to say who is better and who is not entirely. However, there are two distinctively different founder mind-sets in this mix—one is here to make a lot of money and run the show, whereas the other is here to solve world problems and do good. We sometimes hear people call it the "founder's dilemma"—can they not be both? Regardless of who they are, there are crucial skills they need to have first to be a founder and then to build a founding team because nothing else matters if you cannot make a product that people want and do it all on your own.

So, if you think about it, while we often classify founders to have only entrepreneurial skills, they are also effectively someone's manager. So, why have we only been training managers to be effective, and Founders/CEOs get a free pass on this? As an executive coach, I've been fortunate enough to work with some great founders. Except none of the conversations started with *"I need help to be a better manager."* Instead, it was always *"Can you help our company's managers be better?"* On one rare occasion, I met a (restless) founder who was candid enough to tell me how he struggled in a CEO role even as a serial entrepreneur because he finally recognized that before starting the company, he had no actual work experience. Although he was solving most of the problems there, he was in despair when his founding employees began to leave due to a lack of leadership. He knew something had to change, starting with himself.

WHO IS A KEEN LEARNER?

Logically, people are born with unique genetic structures, so they're initially better than others at different things. But Keen Learners are those willing to learn further beyond today, specifically someone with a growth mindset. They believe their talents can be developed through hard work and input from others, not taking for granted that they can be innate. They are different from fixed mindset people who genuinely believe there is no way to develop intelligence or skills. It has become so important that it has evolved into an early education syllabus for children as young as 10. Start young, they said, as "Kids learn by believing everyone can get there."

In this context, we'll look at founders who have not done this before but have somewhat shown that they can by learning. We're talking about first-time founders who are willing in so many marvelous ways and, of course, those who aren't.

Many books, articles, and guides are available for aspiring founders. Search for topics that include Must-Have Skills for Startup Founders; Top 10 Guide to Starting a Company, by serial entrepreneurs; or "How to Find the Right Co-Founder" by accelerators like *Y-Combinators* for example.

These are helpful and readily available guides, except when you're doing this for the first time, and you have yet to find out your actual gaps before going through the whole ordeal of read-apply-reflect. *"Can you learn from others' experience?"* is the bigger question here.

The other elephant in the room is do we even understand why some founders behave the way they do when it isn't working out? Anyone who has picked up a business book on entrepreneurship, or leadership, to generalize, would have seen that the most common themes in becoming a good leader are empathy, creativity, flexibility, and plenty more. Now, this is easier said than done, right?

I believe that Founders simply cannot be expected to read a "Top 10 Must-Have Skills for Entrepreneurship" article and magically turn into one of tomorrow's best leaders. Instead, they are expected to be on a journey to learn what fits their leadership style and how they amplify the good and curtail the bad. That's all there is to it. Except for what we, and I mean peers, investors, and employees, while looking for the good in them, we refuse to accept their gaps, which creates the type of leaders who can't seem to please anyone. You can't know what you don't know, and it doesn't matter how much you read about it.

WILLINGNESS TO LEARN

By definition, you can't study to be a first-time founder. You learn entrepreneurship by doing it and constantly learning from those around you and the experiences that come and go. Learning is critical to this success because you're expected to innovate to stay ahead of your competitors, if not navigate through the uncertainties of a startup.

So, the willingness to learn about things that maybe aren't so glamorous, just like how often a startup is just a slog of doing a lot of tedious work to get to the end goal, should have been the responsibility of every founder from the early stages. For example, simply creating some kind of knowledge map to tell themselves about what they know, what they don't know, and what they should know at that stage would have been a much-needed kickstart for founders to create great companies in the end. What is essential then is also to figure out your mechanism of learning. How do you learn? Do you have a strategy? Do you have a learning style? Is it through visuals? Reading? Community support? Or simply learning by failing?

Our willingness to learn is a crucial behavior that helps us get on in life while growing in every stage. So perhaps, this too can be a guide to first-time founders. Let's see.

WILLINGNESS TO TAKE FEEDBACK AND SUPPORT IN RETURN

When founders are able and willing to receive feedback, they ask themselves how they can continue to elevate their leadership quality every single time. You'll often hear from these founders that they are prepared to listen to the criticisms (although not all at once) because they want to reflect on these points and commit to making a change. It helps them take a step forward in asking for help after.

Contentsquare is a French startup founded in 2016 that tracks customer interaction on their client's websites while analyzing their content performance. The company was led by a first-time Founder/ CEO **Jonathan Cherki**, who created an active feedback loop for its employees. I spoke to **Marisa Bryan,** current VP of Talent Acquisition, to get her insights on how effective this was in building their transparency culture.

How was this feedback loop set up, and in what format?

"In other companies, I've seen examples of CEOs running fire-side chats or Q&A with their leadership teams, most of the time questions would either be vetoed before they knew it and they would hardly be in a real 'live' setting. Our CEO would answer these questions live (in a town hall) and even sometimes quite personal. He didn't shy away from it and took on challenging questions because transparency was key to him. Maybe yes, there were times he didn't have an answer for it, or it wasn't his forte, so he told us he'd find the answers and tell us the next day. It's just such a different energy being in a culture that has the willingness to be vulnerable."

In your opinion, how did he do this so openly, and what did you learn from it?

"I would say that he is genuine and authentic, and it set the tone for the whole company. What I've enjoyed about working here is that nobody has to show off. People are genuinely themselves, and we're open with each other (to a certain extent personally). Because of that, we have conversations and work together to fix things. I find it so much more productive, and you get more delivery from your people in a good way. Because they're not devoting 20 percent of their energy pretending to set an example. We're not in investment banks where everybody's wearing the right suit, going to the right gym, drinking at the right bars, and everything in between. We're told not to waste time figuring how to fit in or playing the role that we're not.

Founders are founders, he is no different from someone who gives directions and can be tough when you're on the wrong side of the decision, but for me, if you can't be humble and lead with compassion and humility, then you'll end up losing staff hand over fist. That's just a waste of everyone's time in the end, right?"

Your leadership team has been evolving and growing bigger each year. Who was the driving force behind this decision?

"Our CEO is always open about how teams should grow; otherwise, the people won't. So, to start, we have a leadership team of people he'd brought in over the years. But increasingly, he's been able to bring more people in to supplement our growth, for example, our CCO, CRO, and most recently, our CMO who has the experience to take us to the next level, and to him, the key point here is constant evolution. For example, I was brought in because of my experience, not despite it. I am told every day they want to learn from someone who has done this before, and because of that, I think we've got diversity right from the start. I think even in the early days, he must have thought fixing this problem five years down the line would be very hard. And to me, this is the testament of just who he is as a leader, not afraid of change. Some very successful startups you see out there are still run by the same five people that 'survived' the evolution. If you don't bring in different points of view, different perspectives, and you're going to go global, it won't work. A global company managed by all French people from day one, can you imagine what that's like? He intended to bring the experts to the table and get people in who could challenge the status quo and challenge them to the way things are done.

When Steve Jobs died, you know, we all genuinely felt sad during my time at Apple. But they also had been actively planning for succession and bringing in people to bolster the team, which just resulted in widening the skill set in the leadership team.

It says a lot about CEOs who are aware they have gaps and actively, intentionally bridge those gaps with those around them. This is why our Q&As were so important to our culture. Because without hearing from what people thought, John would have easily been stuck in the ivory tower, and that's not what he wanted either. So, I think it's a win-win for both sides."

Before we concluded our discussion, she raised a point that has stuck with me since.

"One day, when your book comes out," she said. "I hope investors will read it and say, *"The human part of a company is more than just a resource."* She isn't wrong. You can have the most amazing product in the world, but if you don't have great people selling them, no one's buying. And products don't build themselves. Great people in these companies are only there because their founders listened to what they needed and gave them that. So, how can all of that not be more important than the bottom line?

WILLINGNESS TO BE VULNERABLE TO FORGE TRUSTS

Vulnerability is a powerful way to support a trusting, positive team culture where employees feel eager to be part of the conversation. Still, we must make sure they feel safe doing so. And we can only achieve this if it is a top-down approach, which means the founder must be able to show vulnerability themselves and set positive expectations from this. Nothing builds trust like a leader who allows their employees to teach them because this creates a favorable situation where the leader admires their subordinates. This would be the most rewarding and empowering thing for our employees. And even if a trust is somehow violated over time, they are also more willing to forgive and make themselves vulnerable once again under renewed conditions.

It's not easy being a first-time CEO but making decisions based on both logic and empathy is rare. This makes tough decisions surface more easily and smoothly. And that, I think, is the key to scaling a business. During this time of growth in startups, I find it common that nobody, including the CEO, wants to have the conversation with the early/founding team that more senior people will be hired because they're afraid of people getting hurt or replaced.

Now, this is why I mentioned that balance is so important here. Once you "lie," the trust is broken. People will leave, and all you have left is a generic scale-up business that has lost its legacy glory. Instead,

CEOs can communicate transparently about why they need different people to take the company to the next level by applying experiences from their pasts, considering that they too have never done this before. Or when they could, too, say to the legacy people who cannot move up just yet that they will work on these development plans together slowly so that no one gets left behind.

I spoke to People & Culture Consultant **Joo Bee Yeow, PhD.**, about her recent work with **Infogrid**, a startup with a mission to make buildings smarter via sensors to control everything from lights to water usage so that they can be greener. She was in charge of amplifying their culture. According to her first six months there, she attributed the main driver of this success to how their first-time Founder/CEO, William Cowell de Gruchy, manifests a culture of trust. Besides having a purpose so powerful, which is their biggest attractor for people to join, she concluded that the people, however, stay for the CEO.

First of all, a bit about yourself.

"A talented person. The sweet spot for me has always been when the business is growing exponent and ready to go exponential. And that's where I usually come in to build the foundation to avoid a future HR that's going to come with that because I've been at a different point of the growth journey. And what I'm trying to engineer is how much we can try not to hit that block if possible so that the path to scaling is as smooth as possible."

Let's talk about the foundation of building trusts. How has your CEO done this without coming across as not genuine?

"This is probably generalizing, but as any person leading a business, you naturally don't want to offend. But being the nice guy means you're also not going to have those hard conversations when it is needed, and, in my experience, they worsen when the pressure to scale increases. And you're suddenly dealing with people leaving the company sooner than you expected. At Infogrid, it's a really good sign that he can have that conversation

quite early on and communicate that message in a very inspirational way because honesty is the behavior that he wants to have in the company. So, if you're able to set expectations, not just for the business but also for the culture, you are consistent. For example, he acknowledged that we were starting to show entitlement behavior in one of the All-Hands (like a Town Hall meeting). Usually, any coach will tell you never to call your people entitled. You might speak in circles only to finally say, this is not what I would like to see. Instead, he turned the narrative to "We're committed to this environment for a long period of time, and this isn't the way we should behave if we want to build this future together.

"By doing that, he encouraged a larger conversation than just about benefits. He'd picked the right words to use and said that as we're releasing benefits, we are also going to do it slowly because it takes time to build the right things. And so, people understood why we do things in a certain way that's unique to us because our CEO is trustworthy. Simple as that."

It sounds like he also considered applying himself to what his employees wanted to hear, so the play is empathy. How can CEOs relate to their people when they sit in their ivory tower?

*"Not just ivory towers, I sometimes feel that they do not stand up to what they truly believe in either. Or what they truly want to say. For example, how many CEOs will say, 'My people are feeling idle, and this is not the behavior we want. How can I help?' You need the skill to be this direct but still connect so that as you speak your mind, people don't end up being defensive. And that one I don't know how to coach, but **this is the part where born leaders are made***.

What the CEO can do is balance transparency and the human element. And when we scale a company, it's quite easy to make the mistake of forcing the company to be transparent that we want it to be adopted quickly, so they will tell you as it is and lead to radical candor gone wrong. Or when you are growing so far, you don't have time to build a relationship so just again force honesty on this other person. Relationships and trust go hand in hand, but they are also one after the other. So, being able to say things in a compassionate way under time constraints is pure gold our CEO has. These are the nuances of human interaction when you're going so fast that it brings enormous risks."

Do you have any other startups in mind that you witnessed doing incredibly well because of the same reasons you stated above?

"Honestly, the thing I will not say is that a company is perfect, and that is normal. I'm sure Netflix is not perfect as well. Some startups have the right foundation for the people and culture. Or some have very clear values that reinforce the culture. But founders, if I can advise, need to know how to make hard decisions and empower others in the company.

Let's take two scenarios. On the right, you have Person A (who is) performing well but not a culture fit and has done many things that poorly impact other people's experience. On the left, Person B performed just okay, but (is) amazing at building the people's side and has a positive impact. Which one would the leader normally let go first? The second one, right?

That's the problem right there. Because you cannot see the quantifiable outcome of performance, and because we cannot quantify, we cannot measure the impact on people. But hopefully, you can see it in the revenue or the new features launcher. Yes, so building the right foundation and making the hard decision at the same time is key to protecting its culture."

When trust doesn't exist, often we see a culture that turns toxic. What part does a founder play in ensuring this doesn't happen even with minimal confidence?

"Founders don't like losing control no matter at what stage, and this is what breaks trust. They have a very clear vision, are ambitious, and can start a business. But when you're scaling, the assumption is that your people's problems are more complex. So, imagine if you compare, you're an individual contributor, and then you grow to become a manager of five people. If you can't let go and you are trying to do the job of your people, you're micromanaging. And no one is impressed by it. But at a CEO level, from an individual contributor suddenly to a leader of hundreds of people, that impact is across the company because you have the power of firing someone or empowering them; there's no in-between.

So, the question is can they learn then? I believe anyone can. And instead of people, time is the enemy in startups. Some leaders are born, some leaders are made. And I know some CEOs are trying their very best to become a better version of themselves. Do you want to be king, or do you want to be rich? But if you try to do this all on your own, you can't be successful. This means you need to build a team, and that requires you to build relationships firsthand."

Can we expect all first-time founders to learn this skill? As well as the goal, we go back to the balancing act. There's a reason they are founders. They are risk-takers. They are ambitious and visionary on the product (and company) that they are building. Many times, be it inexperienced or serial entrepreneurs, it is still common to find them without the experience of building an organization. While they know they are learning as they go, they have two choices; do it on their own and make mistakes along the way or hire an executive team to execute it. But how will a founder balance their wishes and give the people what they want? Or will this be the crux of the problem in the future? I hope not.

THE WILLINGNESS TO LEARN FROM OTHERS

Learning from others is a way of social learning, where it has to do with the people around us. You know from the guidance of other masters in our surroundings. Still, the key here is that learning from others depends heavily on integrating our own and others' experiences. We have to compare these experiences and find commonalities to relate them to our situations.

The first-time founders I've worked with have always been interesting because they haven't yet had the opportunity to learn from their mistakes. So, learning from others becomes their superpower. But if they have worked in startups before, they sometimes may have a head start others don't. They learned from the founders of that business. And they often take those learnings. Equally, I've worked with multiple founders who have come out of startups that haven't had great founders and then worked hard to build a different kind of business. First-time founders can be extraordinarily successful but deeply dependent on their background.

On the other hand, thriving cultures can be unsuccessful. Generally, they carry an investment bank or a large consultancy's influence where their perception of performance is based on the experience they've had in those businesses. It doesn't mean they can't be successful, but they're often the ones that take longer to learn compared to coming in with a clean slate.

Throughout the research I've conducted for this book, one startup was regularly mentioned. Without hesitation, employees and consultants described it as a company with an incredible first-time Founder/CEO. I reached out to one of their early employees to get a deeper insight into whether this was a myth or they simply hit the jackpot with their founders.

"Oh yes, our CEO Hanno Renner is an amazing person through and through. And believe me, when I say this is different from the (many) rodeos I had in the other startups. . . ," **Ben Kiziltug**, Head of Northern Europe at **Personio**, began our dialogue.

Tell me more.

"Respectable and impressive CEO, that's how I'd describe him, and I'm not just saying this because I've been here since forever but because he hasn't changed despite our evolution. (Personio's valuation in recent Series E rose to $6.3 billion, making it one of the most valuable startups in Europe since it started in 2014 with only 20 people.) We all talk about it, right? He's got zero experience in starting a company but managed to stay credible and created this type of work ethic that I think is perfect for fast growth. But one of the most impressive things I found is his level of empathy and the way that he deals with almost everyone. He openly says he wants to learn from all of us, all the time.

I'm sure we've all worked with founders who are a bit like, 'Look at me, everyone does exactly as I say with power.' He's the opposite of that. Whenever he comes in, he stops and talks to everyone regardless of their job, and he has an open policy that makes everyone feel appreciated, that they're part of something here. I think that's an uncommon quality, and people generally love working with him and going the extra mile for the company.

As far as I know, he is learning from everyone, including our employees and investors, and he's gained quite a reputation in the community for being supportive. So sometimes, I'm thinking, is there anything else he isn't doing?"

I heard that your CEO makes time to be part of the interview for every person. Is that still the case?

"He tries yes, but because he's just got this passion with people and understanding that he wants to build a company with people who he could do things with together for the right reason, not just anybody who wants to be in a startup, which is such a buzzword right now. So, he is in interviews to make sure he meets all

these people very early on to be our filter, too and to weed out anyone we should worry about from a cultural perspective."

As an employee, what do you feel you gain when you're in a culture like that?

"I think, first of all, it makes you go beyond what's expected because you feel that he's on your side and that he's working with you to understand you as an individual. He tries to understand the person behind the position, which is the opposite of many founders who quickly put people into ROI buckets. What are they doing, and how are they adding value to a company? With Hanno, he gets to know the human being. So, when it comes to those tough times because you always have tough times and relentless periods in a startup, it keeps people in faith, which is very motivating, at least from my perspective.

We've had times when he would just join a sales call with my team to learn from us and, if not, be there to support the deal not because he didn't trust us but because he wants us to succeed together. That's volumes compared to so many founders I've met."

Listening to how Ben described his last four years seemed to be a vision most of us could only dream of, including me. But one thing I learned from this is that founders probably need to be constantly reminded of the importance of these things and given a nudge and prompts to remind them of the things they could be doing or thinking about. So, I think it's helpful for founders to have a mechanism by which they can talk to other founders who may be in similar positions as they share their moments and experiences besides competition because it's becoming relatively easy to start a business these days. And these founders who got it right are probably just giving it a go at the start, so let's help them leverage all of the fantastic tools and resources out there, including themselves.

THE UNWILLINGNESS BECAUSE OF EGO

We all know ego is a common denominator for toxicity in a startup culture. Research has shown that ego is responsible for many negative human behaviors, including being judgmental, manipulative, and constantly feeling superior to everyone around them. They become unwilling to listen to advice and often assert their achievements over others, which ultimately makes them lousy leaders if they are running a company.

But ego can come in different forms, for example stemming from the fear of failure. People in this state are irrational and live with a persistent fear of failing. Simply put, if they are afraid of failure, they will either avoid doing anything at all, or the fear triggers a controlling action that ensures others feel more worthless than they are to avoid experiencing that shame themselves. It manifests in different questions for these individuals, such as "What if I fail and lose everything?"

Founders are people who can tell the story, passionate about the business they're building. And that always helped them get what they wanted. They were able to effectively articulate what they were trying to achieve to both investors and their employees. Typically, they can build good people around them if they're genuinely self-aware. But if they let their ego get in the way, they conflict with how to behave versus what they want. And this is typical behavior in founders that stalk the world of entrepreneurship when they claim they don't know where this 'toxic culture' came from. When they find failure threatening, they choose to tune out because it's easier. As a result, they stop learning.

Zebra Fuel was a startup set up in 2016 in the UK by founders **Bennis and Romain Saint Guilhem**, who had a mission to make our world greener, another startup with a social mission. While it may have been a more complex ecosystem due to regulations, this company didn't fail because of that. They failed because the founders failed. An early employee commented, Massimo[1] took a deep breath before he

---

[1]Massimo was one of the early employees of Zebra Fuel who remains anonymous.

got ready to divulge all the reasons the company went up in flames until the day they shut the business down."

Describe the evolution of the company.

"I joined at the seed stage, and we were about 20-25 people. In the beginning, it was great because there was room for innovation, and we worked closely with all the teams and the founders. Over the period after closing Series A, it became a really tough place to work. These were first-time founders. They had started this right after university with zero working experience and probably a couple of million in the bank. Which isn't always a bad thing, but they didn't want advice from anyone. No one could tell them how to take us up a notch, hire better people for the next stages, and it got to a point where our investors were telling us what we needed to be doing from a day-by-day point of view. In the meantime, one of the founders gave us the impression that they don't feel like working anymore. And as soon as he lost interest in the company, all of us were doing what he should have been doing; run pitch meetings and raise money. He was the CEO, by the way. While sales were slow, the hardest part for me was watching everyone work hard to sustain the company when the founders were the least interested. It made us wonder why we were there.

We got to the point where, upon advice, he was refusing to step down, and that's when I knew this was the end for us. He was advised to keep his shares but bring an experienced CEO to grow the business as a solution. Instead, he said no and kept us all (leadership team included) in the dark until we finally had one month left of the runway. He called an urgent meeting one morning and told us we had to shut down because funding wouldn't come through for another six months. This is the problem for me mostly. I've worked with founders seeking high and low for bridge funds, but he wasn't prepared to do anything remotely close to that. The writings were on the wall from the day we closed our first round."

What do you think was the one thing that killed the company?

"It's like a blend of unwillingness to learn and change, to be honest. Because of their ego, they weren't interested in having someone else teach them how to do things better. They didn't even want to realize that you know what, I have no experience whatsoever, so let me move on and do something else in life. We had great Investors who would have been ready to invest in coaching them. Don't just sit there and think that you know everything. Nobody knows everything. So yeah, ego got the better of them, and it's just a shame overall."

Learning from this experience, do you think as founders, we can do anything to avoid getting into a similar situation?

"Absolutely. If you are a founder, I would say surround yourself with people who have done this before. Ask for help. Leave your ego aside and just be open to grabbing information as much as you can from people and learn from people's mistakes. Try not to repeat mistakes that others made before.

And as for job seekers looking to go into startups, definitely investigate when speaking to the founders in the hiring process. Then try to validate those findings with someone else working there. I would also go as far as looking for founders who have done this at least once. Because if you don't have the experience and you join a team of founders who've never done it too, chances are it's not going to succeed. But maybe failing is good as long as you learn a lot from it. But if that's not what you want to experience, join a founder who at least is willing to learn from anyone but themselves."

Low ego founders typically become ones that I would say are more successful (in the context of being a better leader). This is especially important for first-time founders because they can recognize that their answers aren't always correct. They probably feel that it's rarely going to be the right answer. So, they surround themselves whether it be investors or their leadership team or whoever can help them deliver their vision and mission. All with low ego as an attribute.

Upon reflection, I realized that I, too, haven't always been objective about the kind of environment I no longer wanted to be in because mentally, that is a difficult thing to do, which is to accept your failure. Equally, these types of founders may have been deeply affected by stress and burnout that caused them to behave in a way they usually wouldn't have. Hence, I call it the evolution investigation. People don't usually turn horrible overnight, and it sounded like Zebra Fuel's founders may have gone through a mental challenge that caused them to reach outside of their norm (I can only assume). Although having said that, if you are working with a founder who is simply by definition a psychopath, then save the trouble and yourself. Trust me; they're out there.

SO KEEN LEARNERS, ARE THEY FOUNDERS, OR ARE THEY LEADERS?

Generally, people are curious about startups, so we are never shy of resources out there (while some may be radical) to help founders. It's helpful to read, but it's not possible to apply them to every startup journey because there's a unique DNA that is the company's building block. Even if the stigma around a startup being a *"risky business"* is still there, more people see this as a second option for a career compared to when you're socially expected to join a big bank or consulting firm after graduation just to be seen as successful.

This evolution gave us founders who have been in business for many years, and they will come with some sort of baggage. They already have an idea of how they believe a good company looks. The other founders who haven't done this before but have a growth mindset are changemakers who want to do things differently. These founders go on to be leaders because they will come into the business with this mindset that we are not in business just to make money.

We're here to serve a purpose, and we will make money simultaneously by helping our people and our customers.

The bottom line is, I aspire to encourage as many of those kinds of founders as possible because that's how we'll change the world. While different founders will be coming at it from different perspectives, they need to admit that they do need support. They do need help. There is that constant learning journey, and I think that's the same for every leader. If you ignore the blind spot or stay complacent and just think that you know everything already, it's difficult to grow. If you don't open yourself to being challenged, which is probably one of the most difficult things to be conscious about, you're not going to get a lot of feedback and stay vulnerable constantly. And only when you do, you're able to have uncomfortable conversations and be intentional about learning and living by the values you want your employees to own. So, it remains a conscious decision on your part to be a teachable leader.

CHAPTER 10

The Black Diamond

CHAPTER 4

The Black Diamond

You may have thought to yourself, "I'm going to read this chapter first." Because everything you've read feels relatable to you, even if only a little bit. So, you want to jump straight into finding out how you can be that perfect founder or meet the ideal leader. When I started writing this book, I had a founder in mind who fit the description in this chapter, but that person turned out to be better for the other chapters. Along the way, I realized that my perception had changed as I learned from others' experiences and war stories. What is a Black Diamond anyway? And is it even important?

The challenge with founders is that their company is so critical that they adore it more than a human child. This is a generalization but also a personal observation. Some founders might put all their time and attention into doing what they believe is right at that time. Because they're the founders, they risk surrounding themselves with people who say what they want to hear. They don't realize that this falsity is often caused by known negative consequences for telling the truth. Consequently, they walk into an "emperor's new clothes" situation where everybody is pretending that the reality is not what it is, including themselves.

That's why there isn't such a thing as the perfect founder. Amidst working for 11 startups in seven years, I've coached four founders and mentored a cohort of 20 at an accelerator. I've also interviewed some wiser, more experienced minds to put together a final letter to founders.

CULTURE NEEDS TO START FROM THE BEGINNING

We know it's challenging to change a culture. It's much easier to build it from the beginning. And whether founders recognize it or not, they are responsible for how the culture turns out. Whether it was intentional or not. For example, while they could be unintentionally creating a culture, they could still be very intentional about what kind of behaviors they find acceptable or not acceptable.

This is why some companies hire people who look like them and have little diversity in perspectives. They will have blind spots that limit innovation although they might find this a most positive environment because when everyone agrees with them, it will feel like the company is aligned. It's fantastic, except the blindness may ignore gaps and confine further growth.

We all look for this environment at work where it's fun, safe, and enjoyable to work in because it's why we get out of bed every day, right? We gravitate towards people that are more like us. It generally feels more harmonious when we're with them. It's easier for founders to build a business primarily with people they like.

The fun begins to wane at a later growth stage if differences aren't introduced intentionally. Most founders tend to frown at this but what is commonly misunderstood here is that being different doesn't mean you don't have things in common.

Naturally, when different people come together, they find commonality, typically the values and purpose that tie into its mission. As we recognize that people are different, we can create that psychological safety where people can be different and express an unorthodox opinion.

They can either be different in physical experiences or express a dissenting opinion and still feel safe to take that risk. That is a sign of a safe culture. So, as the company scales and grows, we'll have to reach outside of our immediate networks, and without diversity, those people will likely not feel very welcome.

They won't necessarily feel like they belong because they were outside the core, which is problematic. Whereas if we were to create this psychological safety, valuing differences, accepting all sorts of vulnerabilities, people become more accessible in the company, creating a culture built on authenticity. We won't blame failing leaders that often if we can help founders recognize the impact of making intentional choices that aren't just an easier way out.

BUILDING COMPLEMENTARY TEAMS ALL THROUGH THIS JOURNEY

While we're searching high and low for the "perfect founder," some believe that they are not born but made. If such a person is perfect on all fronts, then it would be a bit sad because they would be building their startup on their own, making the role lonelier than it already is.

In my experience, better founders can create founding teams that complement each other. Also, it doesn't make sense for a founder to be looking after everything themselves, although to a certain extent, some micromanaging is necessary. If you are a solo founder, you should make it a priority to put a team in place early to support you. This will create the best chances for your startup to succeed.

Identifying early on, whether it's in the quality of co-founders or any employees, is a sign of someone who knows about their weaknesses and seeks advice around that by hiring people who can help them. Bringing people together can foster this willingness to go further and beyond when compensation or other tangible values can be realized. The vision alone is a big part of giving a startup its best chance.

We know that one of the most amazing things for a career is when people **get to work with great colleagues**. Yes, people want to be paid fairly, too. But I keep coming back to this example that people are constantly evaluating the caliber of the team around them. Why? Because we're passionate about what we do, especially in a startup. We want to learn, and when we work with a group of people who want the same things, we're looking forward to seeing them because we know that we're going to do exciting work together and learn from each other's perspectives. It's so much fun to be part of that creative energy.

As founders or the leadership team, you have that collective responsibility for the culture of the business because each one of you should embed these values and radiate them through teams as you're building great teams to work together.

You're always looking around the table for that expertize and potential so that, as a CEO, you can consistently focus on creating something better. And it's a hard and lonely job for the CEO because you continuously have to think about who you can talk to and who you can trust. Think about it: Whoever is talking to you will always be aware that you control their employment, salary, and bonus, so how much honesty do you get, right?

So, you end up in that bubble where people will always say what you want to hear, just like how the Queen smells fresh paint everywhere she goes. And that's the danger if you don't have a team that complements the CEO as radical candor is so overused nowadays because it simply cannot work in real life, especially in a work environment. So, what do you do? To get her views on how she built early-stage teams, I spoke to **Sophie Guibaud**, a seasoned, reputable leader in startups for more than a decade.

What's the first thing we need to know?

"I'd say recognize the environment first. Every one of them is unique to the startup. When the environment in which you're performing or seeking to maximize performance is shifting so rapidly, it's about drawing the team's potential as much as it is about their performance. Because they have to respond to the change in the environment and go through in terms of entering the market, dealing with challenges from new competitors, disrupting the old ways of working. So, it's always about the ability to adapt and shift that you want to find in a team."

When we talked about founders needing to recognize their gaps before building a complementary team, is there any way they can do this well?

"First of all, it's not the founder's job to run an entire business. And it is also not on one person to fix the culture. The culture feels like a community, so to start, if we all are self-aware enough that we are all equally responsible for making this place a great place to work, then we're halfway there. Because as founders start setting examples and defining values you need to live by, they also need to be the first representative of those values because they're not something written about without exercise.

It's okay not to be okay, for example, creating this culture where there's room to fail and continue to try. I think it's really about writing those key principles to show that this is a safe environment, it's okay to make mistakes. Errors lead to being ready to do things better because when we fail, we learn. In my opinion, this is the role of the founder. This is someone that has a vision and can bring it from zero to one by bringing the best people together with a plan of progress. Following that, they might progress to understand the people around them to make up for their weaknesses so that it's a full circle.

Companies need to understand that culture results from founders and leadership behaviors. So, if we have a founder who prioritizes his company over everyone else while it makes sense, the imbalance of this action causes more damage than you can anticipate. So, if the founder recognizes they need help in whatever form they see fit, then at least we can start having the opportunity to swap the sole dependency out."

THE ROLE OF THE PEOPLE LEADER

Another thing about having leadership teams complement each other is that the People/HR team is crucial to building great cultures. The misperception around the role of the People/HR Leader in a startup is a person commonly asked to come in and "fix" a specific culture problem or outrageously asked to 'build' a culture. **Kelly Jackson**, Chief People Officer at **Luno**, tells me how she navigates through this confusion and finds the right partners to "shape" culture together in the UK startup.

Do you have a secret sauce to help founders understand this is a journey together, as a team?

"As you know, the misperception is not unique to one company. It's just an expectation now in all startups that if I'm the People leader, I have the answers to everything. But how I shape my relationships and communication at the beginning is key. For example, suppose they disagree with me. In that case, that bears no relation to me as a human being because if I was desperate to have people like me, so I bend and shape into whatever I think that other person wants, then I'm not a good partner for the

business. If you're comfortable with yourself and realize your worth, you can be more honest with that founder, although they hold power by default. People appreciate honesty more than anything else. So, do I have a secret sauce? No, but I prefer honesty. You have to be clear about what you want your brand to look like, what you say, and how you say it.

In Luno, Marcus (Founder/CEO) is the most significant external thinker. My feedback is that he needs to be super clear about whether he's just spit balling an idea, feedback on something, or whether there is an instruction or a direction. My job is to make sure I can interpret his communication to the people. Otherwise, they will take it all as instruction and go scattering off spending enormous amounts of energy and time doing something that may not be important. For a business to succeed, people have to be aligned with what the company is attempting to accomplish. And they need to have the time to prioritize working on the most important things. And as your business scales, as the CEO, you have the potential to positively amplify that, or create complete chaos if not careful."

That leads to why most people find it challenging to work with founders. Why do you think founders are "difficult?"

"Most of them, particularly in the startup world, have never done it before. And if you think about where they're coming from, although many of them wouldn't admit it, they're probably coming from a place of fear themselves because they're operating massively outside their comfort zone. So, the behavior that can come out is usually coming from a place of fear and trying to compensate and pretend that they're in control or worse, pretending that they know better than everybody else. So, you get this narcissistic behavior that isn't easy to work with.

But going back to how I do this role and for other people leaders out there, having the ability to hold yourself to your moral compass and your values, you'll be able to project where that founder is coming from and help others understand. At the end of the day, they just deeply care about the business that they're creating. Most of them have started it because, at some point, they genuinely thought they could do good for society or the customer. Very rarely by the encounter, they think, 'I'm going to start this business to become a millionaire.' If you appreciate the deep sense of purpose behind it and that they genuinely don't know what they don't know because it's the first time they've done this, help them. That's how I see it. Because I listened, I was able to shape that relationship."

SETTING THE RIGHT TONE FROM THE START

If you have read the actual evolution of **Wework's** rise and fall by Adam Neumann in the infamous *The Cult of We: Wework, Adam Neumann, and the Great Startup Delusion* by Elliot Brown, you would know that Wework wasn't unsuccessful because of its app, which was hardly there, or their outrageous per square meter prices. Their failure was due to their founder's ability to tell the story using terms, tones, languages, and immersion into the idea of tech startups, as opposed to it just really being another real estate company.

There's something about the emotion founders create or not, which can put them on the map in this noisy space. There is also an element of following up on that reputation and setting a tone that can create a community almost out of thin air. Sometimes, their branding can be much louder than the product or the technology, which sometimes isn't a lot.

SO, CAN CULTURE BE A CULT?

Some may even argue that a cult culture can be good for a company. As described by an ex-Apple employee in earlier chapters, she was proud of Apple being a cult culture. Employees carry the brand on their shoulders and will never forget how proud they are to be a part of it all, regardless of what outsiders have to say.

Apple created a culture that purposely mimicked a cult where every employee would know all the products from an end-to-end basis. All employees know their products inside out, no matter their role. But it becomes impossible if you try to apply this to another company that doesn't have a cult vibe. That's where the chain breaks.

A founder looking from the outside contemplating whether they should be intentionally creating this type of culture should first ask if this is their authentic self. Ask if this is the lifestyle you would like, the variety of behaviors my co-workers will have, the interactions you would have with your employees in the future.

Having self-awareness in shaping your identity is another crucial factor to being authentic about what kind of founder you want to be. Founders spend too much time trying to become someone they are not because it doesn't fit the expectations of the mold. If they aren't surrounded by better people and in the areas where they're weaker, they can't succeed. Founders surround themselves with people who aren't as good as them because they want to be the best. That's not how to win. It isn't realistic.

So, being able to bring their authentic self to the table is critical in what we believe defines a good company leader. I discussed the intricacies of using self-awareness to represent an authentic identity with **Marissa Ellis**, the founder of **Diversily**, a consultancy startup focused on helping business leaders drive meaningful, strategic, and inclusive change beyond their company centered around Diversity & Inclusion. She explained how it is from a founder's point of view.

The perfect founder, do they exist?

"I don't believe there is a mold for a perfect founder. I think there are many different types of founders who are fantastic in their ways, but there are traits that great founders have in common. Truly authentic founders can't all be the same, as we are all unique individuals.

"To be authentic, you need to be self-aware. There are two types of people in the world; people who believe that they are self-aware and people who are self-aware. Essentially, no one says they're not self-aware. We all think we know ourselves. The truth is that self-awareness is a lifelong quest. We don't spend enough time getting to know ourselves and self-reflecting. As a founder, you will do your greatest work and have the most significant impact if you are true to yourself.

This means knowing who you are. If you haven't spent the time understanding your motivations, passions, and purpose, you won't be fully clear about your aspirations, strengths, and weaknesses. You also need to understand your limiting beliefs, blind spots, and what risks you're prepared to take. Deep self-awareness is required to grow into the best versions of ourselves. For many, especially those from underrepresented groups, this also means overcoming stereotypes and other people's expectations and judgments.

Founders at the end of the day are just like you and me. However, it is easy to lose track of who they really are and what's important with the pressures and stress of running a startup. Founders that connect to a deeper purpose and live their values can more easily navigate the constant change, decisions, and challenges that they face. Work is no longer a transaction of time for money. People don't just want a job; they want to be part of a positive mission where they feel like they truly belong and are valued."

Is there a way they can learn all of this from the beginning before it's too late?

"I believe it starts from changing the basic conversations we (founders) have. If we just talk about the work that needs to be done and never about how we feel and our principles, then we

*don't create an underlying solid foundation for team suc-
cess. Clarity of purpose, core values, and vision will guide you on
this journey.*

*And let me say this: you're always struggling with time. You will
never have enough time to do everything you need to do. Lack of
time is really about prioritization. You have to be intentional
about making space and time for what you know is important,
such as building the right culture. It is much harder to change a
culture than get it right from the start. The tone set by a founder
will influence how everyone else behaves. This is why self-
awareness, connecting to a deeper purpose, and being intentional about culture are important for founders.*

Nina Mohanty, CEO, and co-founder of **Bloom Money** (a Fin-
Tech startup in the UK that serves migrant communities), attributes
some of her experiences in previous toxic cultures to why she wants to
be a founder. Her goals are to lead with humility and grace to empower
those around her, including her team.

**How did old experiences shift the way you view lead-
ership now?**

*"I remember how unjustly I was treated at a startup a few years
ago. I had been there for a while, and the way it happened stuck
with me for a long time. It left me feeling confused, unfairly
treated, and disrespected. Drawing back on my experience
working in startups, I was always happy to work long hours for
leaders I respected. They didn't necessarily have to be super lik-
able, but they always treated people fairly. And that's the type of
leader I want to be.*

*It's incredibly difficult to respect someone you feel does not
respect you. And unfortunately, that is something that one
encounters a lot in fast-growing startups. People often joke that
founders have to be slightly sociopathic or abnormal to
pursue entrepreneurship vigorously. They're sparkling when the*

cameras are turned on, and they bring their charismatic self forward but as soon as you turn around, they are the opposite. I've worked for a founder who would walk into the office with a 'Why am I here? I don't need to be here. I'm rich' vibe. That type of behavior never sat well with me. Thank you for making it clear that you do not respect any of the people making you rich. There has to be a balance. You must have a certain degree of humility to lead.

Before working in startups, I worked at the US Embassy under the Obama administration. I learned that you could achieve things together with humility. President Obama is well known to be the type of person who treats every person with respect. That's something my parents instilled in me from an early age. It costs nothing to be kind. Because you never know who someone is, what their story is. So many companies have lost people because the founders or leadership were not valuing their expertize, their contributions. In many cases, great talent leaves because of a simple lack of respect."

How would you show you value people, and not just for the sake of show?

"I ask myself questions like how do I get people to be motivated? How do I get them to perform well? How do I retain talent? How do I create a culture that people want to stick around? One of the things we talked about in the startup context was a founder sets the cultural tone, right? I'm thinking about things like, if I want to hire an intern, it's important to me to pay that intern because I want that person to feel that their work is valued. But I also want people who would not typically be able to work for free to seize the opportunity as well.

There are other important questions that founders should think about. What does it look like to celebrate wins? What does it look like to break hard news? Perhaps I'm getting ahead of myself, but these are things that are important because I've experienced them painfully when they go wrong. Not everything's peachy and fine. I understand the need for not disclosing a certain amount of information because it can affect morale and motivation, but if you don't communicate anything at all, how does that affect your business and how people are working?

I also think there are more subtle ways to make people feel valued. Sometimes asking for someone's opinion can make a huge difference. Early on in my career, I was in a meeting, and a department head asked me, 'What do you think? I'm curious about your perspective.' And I may have been spouting absolute nonsense, but he made me feel like he cared about my perspective. The act of calling on me to bring me into the conversation was incredibly valuable to me. Interactions like this have given me the confidence to be in this industry. It's little things like feeling like your expertize is useful and appreciated that have given me the courage to start my own company."

DIFFERENT PEOPLE ARE NEEDED AT DIFFERENT PHASES OF GROWTH

This essentially means there are different needs for the founder, being the company's leader. In the early stages, a sales-driven CEO is needed to take the company from zero to 100. But soon after, an operational leader is much more valuable. At the early stage, CEOs are founders because either it's not that time yet to bring in someone who can run businesses or that they own the idea of the company. In contrast, repeatable successes in generating revenue, getting the product off the ground, pivoting the go-to-market strategy all come down to whether this CEO can execute with a team behind them. That's why we call them the operator sometimes, and seasoned CEOs are not just a "good-to-have" these days. A more cynical view is that later-stage CEOs are groomed to take over as the founder steps aside while letting someone else be the figurehead for the company.

Tim Pointer, Chief People Officer of **CAA-GBG Global Brand Management Group** and long-time veteran of building cultures in startups of different sizes over the years fed my curiosity of the why.

In your experience, why do we need a different type of founder at different phases?

"Having seen a number of businesses at different stages, I don't believe in perfection in founders. Even if someone is super well suited for today, they might not be for tomorrow. So, I look at it as depending on the phase the business is in and what it requires from the founder: the business's growth stage, the stakeholder relationships; the vision and strategic plan; creating and sustaining a business culture, the alignment of resources with clarity and focus. Someone may have a particular strength for funding rounds, selling the opportunity to the external stakeholders. Or she may be exceptional in creating that sense of purpose and drive within the founding team, like lightning in a bottle. But often, founders may not be as well suited for the follow-up phases where they are now needed to manage at a different pace, ensure global governance, or lead across a breadth of geographies, time zones, and cultures. It's a completely different energy to lead a more mature business."

Approving the thoughts of Tim that these different skills are needed for various stages of growth, as an early-stage investor, **Yi Luo** is of the opinion that these skills are rare and new founders need to be coached.

It's been said, we're all looking for that Founder/CEO who can lead the business for a long time, but we also know that it requires different skills because if not done right, culture and brand start to get affected even if they are great in the early days. How do you know when you've got a founder who can avoid this?

"In my experience, I think because I'm a pre-seed investor, I care about the preface of founders. I think it's really hard to assess in

the early days, and sometimes you may be in luck, but it's not guaranteed. If they have the ability to learn and adapt, then entrepreneurship is absolutely for them in the long run. Although not everyone can do so. Many founders can either do 10 to 100, and the probability is less than 1 percent for those who can go from zero to 100. And as they scale the business where they are managing a team of a thousand people, they need to pivot and start caring about the people around the revenues. In my case, when assessing pre-seeds, I ask questions like 'Are you able to build something when you reach a seed-stage with this capability?'"

As an investor, what commonality do you look for in a founder that perhaps can run through different stages?

"Although it's going to be a very long list of what I find as criteria in a good founder, I tend to see a couple of common behaviors. The most important one being, the founder has an extreme mission-driven approach. I mean, it's not just like the founder will always come out with a mission. But you can tell that it's different if they were genuinely passionate about the task, then they will be able to solve the problem. This way, I know they will get through the toughest period. Resilience is always important too. I recently met a founder who is building a biotech startup, and the problem he is trying to solve comes from him battling this condition himself. So, through the whole journey, he represents the problem and the solution in the best pitch possible. That, to me, is what every founder should learn.

Another thing I think is vital is their execution speed in every stage. When it comes to the actual business, there are a bunch of founders who would just go non-stop. They never stop, and sometimes it can be difficult for their employees to keep up with that pace. They try different things and push the boundary and limits with higher speed each time. Some say it's bad because you burn people out, but that's why they need to have a better leadership team instead of the founder changing. Because I think this type of founder has a better chance to win the market because, with speed, they also have the chance to test it quickly, correct themselves, and move forward. If you see somebody like this with a vital mission and resilience, they can execute quickly. Even though there's a problem or a mistake, they could go around it.

On top of that, if they can influence people, they can mobilize people worldwide to bring brilliant talent along their journey. Especially important in the early stages, where you almost have nothing to show, is bringing on the world's best talent.

What I am describing is also a very rare founder."

WILLINGNESS TO BE ONE TRUE SELF

Whenever I get confused about why people behave a certain way, I lean my prying on **Ruth Penfold** (a personal confidante, a seasoned startup People leader, and now, a life coach) as she explained the inner workings of some founder behaviors. We broke down the psychology behind why they behave a certain way.

Startups can be brutal some days. When the founder asks you to do something that doesn't align with your moral compass, or sometimes it's just not trivial because they should not have done it this way. You find yourself standing up for your beliefs at the very start of this exciting job but quickly starting to feel the gravity pulling your shoulders lower and lower until one day, you stopped asking the questions altogether.

We tell ourselves that it is safer to put up a façade of conformity in these situations, where we mute our divergent standpoints. We smile when there needs to be a smile, we frown when there needs to be a frown, and we nod when there needs to be a nod—all to avoid the disagreement that may make those days even harder than they are.

Unfortunately, when we put up this type of façade, it also creates a sense of conflict in our perceptions, subsequently causing symptoms

of depression. Soon we find ourselves less engaged and less committed to the company, with more intentions to leave. That's the irony of
it all; because we have been pretending to fit in, we eventually make
up our mind that we don't want to.

**Being your authentic self sounds like an easy thing to do,
but I know it probably isn't. Why is that so? Is this what differ-
entiates good versus flawed founders?**

*"Everybody, all of us, is the product of what we learned about
ourselves when we were young, the world, and about how we fit
into it. Much of the personality that we have individually created
is borne out of coping mechanisms—namely, if I act like X, I get
Y reaction from another person.*

*The way that we condition ourselves in the world is therefore so
insidious. It is nearly impossible to be our true selves because we
will never know who that is. Instead, we can learn who we are,
why we are the way we are, and develop a true sense of self that
means that we become aware of our reactions to things and the
impact of those reactions on others around us.*

*The challenge with founders, though, is that they're trying to do
something genuinely courageous. That is to build something that
steps beyond the realms of normal human comfort zones.*

*Doing so means that they are operating in a superhuman way
most of the time, with long hours and conflicting priorities, and
therefore they don't have the time for this kind of deep work, even
if they have the desire to do so. Unfortunately, this kind of deep
personal work is the key to creating a more supportive dynamic
amongst teams where we all feel like we have the space to thrive
and truly belong.*

*Instead, we often have leaders who believe that the way they
experience their company is how everybody else does. They don't
realize that what feels like a healthy culture can be a harsh*

environment for others. If they challenge a lot to create the best possible product, the reality might be that their challenge is confronting others in an unsafe way.

When we don't feel safe, that's when we stop feeling able to share our ideas and our truer sense of self with the world.

Therefore, the hard learning for leaders is that, even if you have the best intentions, you can't just be who you are without considering your impact on others. If you want to build a business that innovates and ideates thought-leading products, you simply have to expend a good deal of energy building the right dynamic with your people."

So, this is self-awareness we're talking about?

"Yes, but it certainly doesn't offer any kind of silver bullet solution. The challenge with radical self-awareness is that the person has to be open to it—which as a Coach, I can tell you only happens to humans genuinely ready to go on that journey.

If you're not ready to shed the layers of deception that you've created around you, then you're not ready. The brain is a clever organ that constructs and makes sense of the world to minimize our pain, most of the time at least. Doing this type of work is painful, so until a person is ready to go there, their brains will always construct reasons to avoid it.

I don't think that there is anything that you can enforce that will make a founder walk that path, but there are gentler ways to support people onto the path of self-awareness if they are open to that."

We say founders are why cultures are toxic, and there's no one else to blame. What's your view on this after operating in these People leader roles?

"I believe that they set the tone, yes but that the group sets the culture of an organization. At the founder level, it's both about what they do and what they don't do. That's the issue here. Some founders can be actively horrible, and when they behave this way and show everyone 'this is how we behave (here),' then either people will leave or start to mirror those behaviors.

In most cases, it's less about active bad behaviors. It is more about the microaggressions of how the company shows up to each other that are ignored. Any small lousy behavior that isn't challenged can easily create a bad culture overall. For founders, if you know this isn't something you are actively interested in, then you need to hire a leadership team that does.

Trying to make your culture sound better than it is doesn't work either. While you can be aspirational in the way you define what your values are, the world will always feel the actual energy of what your culture is rather than what you might want it to be.

Again, founders and leaders need to be careful not to assume that other people have the same experience of their organization. Listening, learning, and humility around other people's experiences of you as a leader will be the key to unlocking the magic that waits for your organization when all of the human beings in it have the space to thrive and truly belong."

THE ABILITY TO SEEK OUT HELP IN STAYING MENTALLY HEALTHY

Mental health refers to the state of our well-being. We recognize it to be our ability to cope with the stresses in life, the conflicts we have to go through, and our interactions with people around us that are either good or bad for us. For founders, this also relates to how well they can make and execute decisions.

Why is it Essential in the Startup World?

Now and then, HR will talk about the mental health of their employees, but no one asks the founders if they are, okay. It's such a simple practice, but it isn't even ingrained in our day-to-day conversations because the startup industry is a problem in itself. Sadly, this is a world dominated by males. That is going to change but compared to women, men, in general, have an issue talking about their mental health. The consequence of having a disproportionate number of males building startups means we don't have enough people breaking this taboo in this ecosystem.

I care about this topic deeply because I've gone through burnout and have spent many years working through therapy and coaching to get to a mental state where I feel comfortable in my skin. I no longer feel the burden of doing the bidding of a poorly behaving founder. But if I flip the coin to the other side, I've learned to understand, mindful I'm not making excuses for it, about why founders behave the way they do, and it has a lot to do with their inability to stay mentally healthy for the journey they're on.

While I have found it very difficult to come to terms with needing help, you have to have the self-awareness to take that first step to use resources and help to push yourself out of that comfort zone. Challenging on its own, it doubles the effort for males because there is still such a stigma around it. It is often also deeply rooted in males not seeking help from someone else, which is why the patriarchy is toxic in this case. Just think about the kind of culture we're creating under this influence.

Upon chance, I was introduced to **Janos Barberis**, an investor, entrepreneur, and the Co-Founder of **Supercharger Ventures** with an established track record in the FinTech industry who is working with Annabelle Cameron, a psychologist in a new project called **Founders Taboo**, which is going to be the world's first free online course for founders' mental health and well-being. The course will be taught by clinical psychologists, entrepreneurs, academics, and investors to raise awareness on the topic, but most importantly, to ensure that Healthier founders create Healthier companies.

Tell me about the project and how it started.

"First of all, this is a costly problem we want to solve. From the top of my head, losses directly linked to founder burnout cost the US VC industry alone over $8 billion a year. This operational risk could be minimized by better investing in founders' well-being and has nothing to do with poor product-market fit or sufficient finances. It simply means the founder, the driver of the vision, crashed.

Founders Taboo has a three-step approach: First, we're building an online course and platform to raise further awareness on the topic. So that founders who face difficulties know that they're not alone, and for those who are not currently experiencing issues, to be aware of those affecting their peers and the ecosystem as a whole.

Second, carry out clinical research with universities to complete a thorough mapping to demonstrate the link between the mental health and well-being of founders and startup outcomes.

Third, we aim to reach a point where we can mandate VCs to have compulsory well-being reporting back to the board. Just like ESG reporting is now mandated to companies, including startups."

How will it work, and what can founders gain from of it?

"Annabelle brings the psychological background, while I bring the entrepreneurial experience. This combination helps us create something that can benefit founders' well-being and life satisfaction and support the healthy functioning of the ecosystem as a whole. The course has been designed to function as a well-informed knowledge, guidance, and resources toolkit.

"It is to be freely accessible for founders online, anytime, anywhere, as we do not want founders to face barriers to well-being support. We have brought together expert speakers from various disciplines, including mental health professionals, academics, executive coaches, well-being solution providers, and industry experts.

The role of these individuals is to speak on a range of important topics from startup-specific pressures to introducing a range of well-being tools and techniques, such as mindfulness, habit monitoring, visualization, EFT tapping, exercise, etc.

The goal is to empower founders through practical guidance from knowledgeable others in the industry to equip themselves with resources that best support their well-being as they navigate the startup journey rollercoaster. Beyond this, we have a section dedicated to founders speaking candidly about their experiences and learnings, and this is where we hope to break down the taboos.

The prevailing stigma around mental health is one where burning out is worn as a badge of honor. However, the lack of awareness and well-designed support for founders makes this 'romantic view' of the startup story a real danger for founders that lack the awareness about the risk and the infrastructure to help them. As with most things, it is certainly a combination of both."

I'm thrilled that you're taking this forward because you're right that we don't talk about it enough. Mental health issues are not unique to startups, but we are left behind because of it. As a rarity, some investors have asked female founders that I know outright if they have a support system because if they're investing in them, they want to know if they have the resilience to get through the tough times. How can we help?

"I mean, starting a movement sounds like a grandiose word, but it takes time to change habits, so I think the more people talk

about it, the more it becomes normal, and the more it becomes normal, the more it will be implemented in practice. That's what we're hoping for. Awareness is the first step for all of us. The industry as a whole, too, needs to change. Having talked to many founders, they almost always put themselves second. Their well-being is not the priority.

They'll prioritize their team, the company, and their obligation towards the company. And so, this is why making it mandatory reporting to the board, similar to ESG mandated reporting, is the long-term goal. We are removing from founders the capacity to put themselves last by creating governance around them."

The startup journey is not easy. Founders navigating without investing time and energy into their well-being and adequate support and resources is creating hardship, which we believe is avoidable. Founder burn-out is not just personal. It is burning billions in VC money each year, both of which are preventable. Founders committing to their well-being is only a piece of the puzzle that needs to be solved. They also must feel comfortable saying when they do so or need help.

They should not fear losing investment or client opportunities because they were open about and investing in their mental health. If investors only see founders as another asset and money-maker, how can we expect founders to prioritize their mental health? We need transparency and open dialogue around mental health in the relationship between founders and stakeholders. Only then can we have a robust ecosystem.

Whether mental health is a precondition for founders' entrepreneurial journey or a result of their company activity, it is hard to argue against the fact that founders are disproportionately affected. Compared to other socioeconomic classes, they are ten times more likely. That's how far the "statistical comparison" should be, especially if you are an investor.

Treating a founder as a portfolio statistic or just an asset that will generate a return dehumanizes them. Doing so has the natural consequence for investors not to look at their founders as humans. In this case, how do you even start to create that open relationship and dialogue around mental health that is so important to startup success? And how do you allow yourself to do it under these pretenses? Second-time founders might have a better chance of breaking this vicious cycle, but that is also a minority.

Investing in a founder's startup doesn't solve the money issue of the founders personally. Personal financial stress, a critical factor in mental health, needs to be openly discussed. If the conversion is difficult or awkward, then elevate it and make it a governance element for the company to commit to invest and report on the founder's well-being.

It's essential to start the conversation now because it will take time. One can meet only so many people every day, week, month, and year. Instead of having ambassadors, online courses, and ecosystem building sharing our message, the impact is multiplied. Today the conversation is about making the startup ecosystem healthier, almost a CSR project at scale. Tomorrow, we hope to discuss the founder and their unique needs, like creating financial return, and sustainable companies. Only then will it be easier for founders to justify how investing in THEM, as people, not assets, will make for a better outcome.

The way I see it is it's so important to start the conversation now because if you're one person, yes, you can make minor changes, but you're also hoping to bring the whole community together. And I do believe that people who are aligned to this conversation forward will create a tremendous impact.

I can only imagine this idea will continue to grow larger and larger, but I would also hope at one point we get to shift the conversation a bit more driven by what people now want to have as part of their lives, not just an atmosphere driven by the market or industry. Change takes time. Let's start from a place where we can.

Closing Reflections

While I have focused most of the book thus far on examples of what has and hasn't worked, there is one important takeaway that still needs to be emphasized. There is not a right or wrong answer here. There is no one way to be a successful Founder/CEO. The only "wrong" is failing to do the right thing by your people.

Founders and CEOs are human. They are not infallible, and they need as much support as any other employee, but perhaps just in a different form. There is a learning curve to starting your own company, and what works for one company or one Founder may not be the right fit for another. That's okay. More than anything, I want this book to be the inspiration to ask the right questions—for Founders and CEOs, as well as for employees—that will help them clarify the direction in which they'd like to go. Whatever role you're in, you won't always get it right on the first try. But in failure, you can also find great success.

There seems to be a terrible misconception that Founders and CEOs just instinctively should know how to build the right type of company culture and that they will make no mistakes. That is just not true, and it's a bit unfair of employees to expect it. Working for a startup means that employees are as much a part of the culture as the Founder/CEO—and in a way that is likely very difficult or almost impossible in larger, more established companies. As an employee, or as an HR professional, you have the power to influence and direct a startup's culture. There are going to be highs and lows in that process, and Founders/CEOs and employees alike should be prepared for that.

More so than any other employee, an HR professional will be instrumental in guiding the Founder/CEO in the creation of the company's culture. People Leads have an obligation to make sure that leadership prioritizes treating employees right. As we've seen throughout our 10 case studies, that is not always the case. To that end, I've created 10 essential questionnaire categories that you can use to determine the foundation of a startup's culture. I use these questions in my own work to this day. For HR professionals, I say this: You will frequently be tasked with building the culture for a startup, or if you are coming in later in the formation of the company, you may be tasked with "fixing it." Either way, you have your work cut out for you, and that is why I recommend you go through this exercise. Don't do it just once either. Check in regularly and see if any of your answers have changed. Carefully consider each one and whether it applies to your company. Once you have identified the problem, you are that much closer to helping your Founder/CEO find the right solution.

While I designed these originally for my own work as an HR professional, they are equally useful for any employee. For Founders/CEOs, you can use this list to do a little soul-searching. Be honest with yourself. *Genuinely try* to recognize yourself in each of these questions and only discard them when you are certain they are not applicable to you or your company. If you are unsure, mark them for review. If you are certain they *do* apply, start addressing the problem *now*. For employees or potential employees, use these questions to assess your job. Are you sure you want to be working for a company, whichever category it falls into? Are you comfortable taking a job with a company that might be struggling with some of these issues? Don't blindly walk into any job with any company. Do your due diligence now.

SAMPLE QUESTIONNAIRE

1. Is there a leadership feedback loop? Is the Founder/CEO hiring friends and family over more qualified individuals? Are they overly fond of their own story/brilliance/culture to the point where they no longer value the input of others? For more established startups, is there a distinct lack of morale and employee engagement in the company?

2. Is the Founder/CEO focused too narrowly on specific qualities in new hires, to the exclusion of qualified candidates. Are they

requiring certain traits without basis for that requirement? For more established startups, is there a noticeable lack of diversity?

3. Do you have more high-profile talent than is strictly necessary, but lack focus on your product or service? Does the Founder/CEO brag about poaching talent from other companies? Are they leaving the creation of company culture solely, or almost solely, to others (like you)? For more established startups, is there more publicity about the team than there is about the product?

4. Does your company have a higher-than-normal turnover? Look around the company: How many of the original employees are still there? Why do people say they left the company? For more established startups, what kind of employee reviews does the company get on sites like Glassdoor?

5. Is your company deadline focused? Is there an element of "drive" within the company? What do customers say about your products and services, especially in comparison to your competition. For more established startups, has the Founder forgotten they are still on a learning/building journey?"

6. How concerned is leadership with being considered "cool" or "anti-establishment"? Is the Founder/CEO too focused on small aspects or processes in the company and neglecting the big picture? Are the majority of employees engaged in the mission? For more established startups, what does the Founder/CEO involve themselves in on a daily basis?

7. Does your company have multiple locations? Are workers allowed to work remotely full-time? How does culture differ between locations and how does it differ for remote workers? As an already more established startup, are leaders discussing "sustainable culture?"

8. Is your company's leadership trying to force culture on their employees? Are they holding "voluntary" (but really mandatory) events? Does your Founder/CEO express how they want everyone to be one big family (or expects everyone to be friends

outside of work)? For more established startups, what kind of employee engagement or enthusiasm for these events is evident?

9. Are your company's employees shooting for the middle or shooting for the stars? Does your Founder/CEO foster an attitude of learning and personal development—from themselves as well as from others? For more established startups, what are the consequences for failing to meet goals? Are they outlined as clearly as the rewards?

10. Does your Founder recognize they don't know everything? Do they seek to surround themselves with others who are smarter or better at specific aspects of the company? Do they have a focus on employee welfare and success? Do they really listen? For more established startups, does the company culture immediately feel like an open and engaging place where other viewpoints are welcomed?

As I'm sure you noticed, each question is associated with a specific type of founder culture that we discussed in this book. Some companies may fit in more than one category. You may also want to add your own questions down the line, but this is a good starting point for you to identify the root culture of a company you are working for or about to work for. Identifying the problem is half the battle, and don't forget—the CEO owns a large percentage of company culture. Any changes have to start at the top.

FINAL NOTE:

We talked a lot in this book about how CEOs impact culture, but to varying degrees, both HR professionals and employees will each own some of it, too. You should be applying some of these lessons to your own work. Every employee is responsible in one way or another for the *soul* of a startup—the way we behave as leaders, the way we promote or discourage workplace behaviors, and the prioritization of well-being, etc. In particular, I want to emphasize the idea of "Always be learning." Never stop having that attitude. Learn from leadership, learn from employees, take classes, do personal and professional development programs, and most of all, actively listen. Make sure you are advocating for this attitude with your colleagues and your leadership. And make sure you come to this job from a place of authenticity. Stand up for your employees and colleagues, and for what is right. Sometimes that's hard. I've experienced that myself—the hard way—and you now have the opportunity to learn those lessons in a far easier way than I did. Working for a startup can be an extremely rewarding experience but it is not without its challenges. I wish you all the luck and success as you navigate your journey into the soul of startup culture.

Acknowledgments

As much as this book started out from the pages of my journal (*cliché, I know*) it was initially taking shape as a rant piece. I shrugged at it. While it wasn't the easiest thing for me to do to bare my scars publicly, I eventually got to a point where the writing healed me, and I started playing back memories in a different, brighter light. Despite my changed mindset, it's the people around me who got me here.

I want to thank my family, and a special dedication to my husband Jonathan, who told me writing isn't as scary as I thought it would be and it would finally be a relief to lift the burden of war stories I dared not share. I'm glad I did. Not only have I been more honest with the people around me, I'm more honest with myself about where my boundaries lie and what else I need to learn in this ever-changing ecosystem. So, this is for you.

I also want to thank those who got me through my days in Revolut and Pollen, you know who you are.

A massive thank you to the founders at 11:FS who gave me a safe haven to learn to be a better leader and made me realize "building cultures" is the thing I'm meant to do. Especially David who always empowered this bruised HR person who could change it all by learning what not to do from my earlier mistakes. And Ross, who over the years sends me words of encouragement whenever I need them.

It's not a surprise to say I'm forever grateful for all the mighty women in FinTech (especially) who always supported, mentored, and generously took the time out of their busy schedules to help me along the way, fighting off one combat after another. And a special thanks to a few, namely Yi, Nim, Vittoria, Merita, Ruth, and Ioana.

I want to thank my team at Oakam for giving me the space while I got through the lockdowns in London writing what I wore on my sleeves. Amber, Andrea, without your cheer that I shouldn't shy away from sharing these learnings or we wouldn't be here today.

And last but not least, the interviewees for being courageous enough to share your stories with me and giving this book the life it needed. Otherwise, this would have just been pages of my moderately enraged experience, which would probably not be of much use to others. I also thank you for connecting me to colleagues, peers, and friends who all have personal stories to share with me because without them, the conversation stops here. Which is not what we want.

About the Author

A reformed engineer, Sophie's expertize is now focused on reinventing talent management for FinTech industries. She is passionate about establishing corporate blueprints for the working culture of the future.

She's led recruitment projects with Ford, General Motors, and IBM, before shifting her passion and focus to setting up the future of HR in startups like Revolut & 11:FS. Via Chief of Stories, an HR and Culture consultancy she founded in 2019, Sophie has worked with over 16 startups (and Venture firms) in Europe, Australasia, and the US. She is a mentor for aspiring founders in startup accelerators and a career coach in the startup community specifically supporting HR newcomers.

As a mental health first aider, Sophie has created a support system to combat depression, anxiety, and other factors specifically affecting rapid-growth businesses. She is widely recognized in the UK for her innovative ways in changing how HR works in tech and is also a regular keynote speaker.

A prolific writer on issues of diversity, Sophie also runs an HR community in Slack, as well as a Work Experience Program for young women. She is an award-winning Diversity and Inclusion professional who has inspired other women to be courageous in championing or fighting for efforts they believe are important to the tech industry. Having been on the Women in FinTech Powerlist for three consecutive years, the first HR professional to win the Top 35 Standout in FinTech in the UK, and most recently one of the top 20 Women in Software Powerlist UK, she is opening doors for conventional HR to be practised in the disruptive world of FinTech.

Index

Accelerators, 79
Accountability:
  balancing values and, 91
  lack of, in creating communities, 132
Acquisitions, 91–92
Actions:
  failure to align mission
    and, 150–152
  of individuals (*see* Behavior(s))
Agussol, Anouk, 154–155
"Air cover," 71, 72
Amazon, 50–52
Ambition, lack of, 86–89, 93
Amoruso, Sophia, 146
Apple, 145, 146, 163, 185–186
Appreciative inquiry, 110
Artificial hierarchies, 98
Asking for opinions, 190
Attwood, Jeff, 138
Authenticity, 162, 180, 186, 207
Authentic self, 186–188, 194–195
Autonomy, 3
  in collectivistic culture, 119
  in individualistic cultures, 125
  providing team with, 71
  and success of startups, 98

Barberis, Janos, 197–200
Bates, Jason, 100
Behavior(s):
  cultures resulting from, 183
  ego-based, 102–109, 172
  and mental health, 197

microaggressive, 196
mimicking, 32
toxic, investors' encouragement of, 17
Benefits to employees:
  free meals, 27–28, 36
  shares schemes, 36
Bezos, Jeff, 79
BitBucket, 138
The Black Diamond, 177–201
  being one's true self, 193–196
  building complementary
    teams, 180–183
  and culture as a cult, 185–190
  need for different people at different
    growth phases, 190–193
  role of people leader, 183–185
  seeking help in staying mentally
    healthy, 196–201
  setting the right tone, 185
  starting culture from the
    beginning, 179–180
Blakely, Sara, 97
Blame culture, 110
Blind spots, 187
Bloom Money, 118–119, 188
Bootstrapping, 80–81
Borisov, Hristo, 119
Boundaries, creating, 28
Brand(s):
  customers' reactions to, 145–146
  derived via communities, 147
  founder's carrying of, 185–186
  importance of people vs.,
    124–125

Breakfasts, free, 27
Breaking hard news, 189–190
Brear, David, 98–100
BrewDog, 45
"Bros club," 17, 39
Brown, Elliot, 185
Bryan, Marisa, 145, 161–164
Bumble, 140
Bureaucracy, 3–4
Burnout:
    with acquisitions, 91–92
    common reasons for, 73
    of employees, 73
    of founders, 200
    of HR professionals, 72
    and mental health, 197

CAA-GBG Global Brand Management
        Group, 191
Cameron, Anabelle, 197–199
Canva, 80
Caring:
    and collectivism, 132
    in communities, 140
    and individualism, 131
    leadership style of, 128–129
Celebrating wins, 189–190
CEOs. See also individual CEOs
    author's advice to, 203–207 (See also
        The Black Diamond; individ-
        ual topics)
    biased decision-making by, 58–59
    company overhauls by, 85–86
    complementary teams for, 180–183
    culture reflecting beliefs of, 25
    for different growth phases, 190–193
    as driver of community, 143–144
    at early stages, 190
    ego-based behaviors of, 104–105
    experience levels of, 89–92
    "hands-off," 80, 82

inexperienced managers as, 17
lack of forward thinking by, 81–82
lack of interest in mission by,
        83–85
later-stage, 190
as managers, 72, 159
micromanagement by, 105–109
people who can be trusted by, 181
sample questionnaire for, 204–206
strategy updates from, 101
without strong ambition, 86–89
Challenging times, pulling together
        during, 90–91
Change:
    adapting to, 182
    in collectivist cultures, 127
    of a culture, 188
    designing, 98–101
    for different points of view, 163
    of directions, 111–113, 149
    unwillingness to, 175
Cherki, Jonathan, 161–163
CityM, 146
Clubhouse, 138
Collaboration:
    in building community, 139–140
    in collectivistic culture, 117
Collateral damage, 71–72
Collectivism:
    culture of, 117–120, 125–128
    de-idealization of, 132–133
    and diversity, 126–127
    individual interests in, 125
    nuances of, 132
The Collectivist vs. The
        Individualist, 115–133
    de-idealization of collectiv-
        ism, 132–133
    misperception of individual-
        ism, 125–132
    as opposites, 120–125
    relationship-like culture, 117–120

Communal work environ-
    ments, 128–132
The Community Builder, 135–156
    anatomy of a community, 139–140
    community that extends a conversa-
        tion, 152–155
    community with a mission, 140–144
    failure to align mission to
        actions, 150–152
    meaning of "community," 137–139
    reliance of startups on communities
        for success, 155–156
    tragically misaligned
        community, 150
    whole community focused around
        the founder/s, 144–150
Company overhauls, 85–86
Complementary teams, 180–183
Conformity, façade of, 193–194
Contentsquare, 161–164
Conversation(s):
    about mental health for
        founders, 201
    among founders, 187–188
    in building trust, 165–166
    community that extends, 152–155
    ignorance of new ways to start, 137
Corporate culture, 1
Corporate hackers, 79. See also
        The Unlearner
Corporations:
    being acquired by, 91–92
    office politics and bureaucracy in, 3–4
Coty Inc., 80
Cowansage, Cadran, 153
Criteo, 58–59
Critical mission, holding on to, 82–85
The Cult of We (Brown), 185
Culture(s). See also Work
        environments
    assessing foundations of, 204–206
    of blame, 110

changing, 188
collectivistic, 117–120, 125–128
and consistent commitment to
        purpose, 101
corporate, 1
as a cult, 185–190
developed by founders, 9–10, 38, 72,
        91, 203 (See also individual
        companies)
of fear, 124
having some control over, 75
individualistic, 72, 121–125,
        128–131
managers' lack of control over, 71
misalignments of, 71–72
mistakes in building, 203
overhauling company to change, 86
of performance, 129–131
responsibility for, 182
separated by geo locations, 139
setting the tone of, 185, 188, 189
started from the beginning,
        179–180
startup, 1, 2
successful, 169
of togetherness, 148
of transparency, 47, 161–163

Decision-making:
    based on both logic and
        empathy, 164
    in collectivistic culture,
        117, 119–120
    in individualistic culture, 121–122,
        128–129
    mentally-healthy, 196–197
    and nepotism, 17
    unjustified, 59
    voices in, 10
De Gruchy, William Cowell, 165–167
Dell, Michael, 79

Development plans, 57–58
Dija, 121–125
Directions, change of, 111–113, 149
Diversity, 10
    and collectivism, 126–127
    and culture creation, 179–180
    dedication to conversation about, 153
    lack of, 23–28, 39
    of leadership teams, 100
    quota for, 15
Diversity (company), 153–154, 186
Due diligence, 120

Ego:
    behaviors based on, 102–109
    forms of, 172
    in founders, 123
    unwillingness to learn because
        of, 172–175
Elemy, 45
11:FS, 80–81, 98–101
Ellis, Marissa, 153–154
ELPHA, 153
Empathy, 164, 166–167, 170
Employees. *See
        also specific topics, e.g.:* Hiring
    achieving happiness of, 20
    average age and tenure of, 19
    being respectful of, 20
    culture impacted by, 206–207
    early-stage vs. late-stage, 76
    lack of support for, 60–63
    managers' responsibility for, 101
    psychological burnout of, 73
    quality of, 181
    rapid increase in number of, 45–48
    valuing, 189–190
Empowering teams, 71
Engagement Leads, 16
Engagers, in communities, 139
Enneagram method, 28–29

Entrepreneurs:
    communities for, 138
    frustrations of, 137
    learning by, 160–161
    perception of, 97
    toxic environments created by, 37
Execution speed, 192–193
Expansion, for the wrong reasons, 59
Extended working hours, 25–28

Facebook, 79
Fadell, Tony, 97
Failure:
    accepting, 175
    to align mission to actions,
        150–152
    fear of, 172
    finding success in, 203
    safe environment for, 104, 182–183
    of startups, reasons for, 102–104
    and tone set, 185
Fairness, 188
Fear:
    of being firing, 20
    culture of, 124
    of failing, 172
    founders coming from a
        place of, 184
Feedback, founder's willingness to
        take, 161–164
"Feel good" companies, 140
Feld, Brad, 138
Fernandez, Jon, 87–89
Fin, 60–63
FinTech, 4
Firings:
    compared to hirings, 45
    fear of, 20
    for not meeting performance
        targets, 30–33
    as red flags, 12

Fixed mindset, 159
Focus:
   from founders, lack of, 73
   on goals, CEOs' loss of, 82
   on growth vs. on founding
      principles, 72
   and support for employees, 60–63
   of teams, 56–58
   of whole community around
      founder/s, 144–150
Forward thinking, lack of, 81–82
Founders, xiii–xiv. *See also specific
      people; specific types of leaders*
   alertness to characteristics of, 40–41
   author's advice to, 20, 203–207
      (*See also individual topics*)
   biased decision-making by, 58–59
   burnout due to lack of
      focus from, 73
   company overhauls by, 85–86
   corporate hackers, 79
   culture developed by, 9–10, 38, 72,
      91, 203 (*See also individual
      companies*)
   culture reflecting beliefs of, 25
   defined, 9
   differences among, 79
   for different growth phases, 190–193
   difficulty in working with, 184–185
   egos of, 102–104
   experience levels of, 89–92
   as managers, 72, 159
   mindsets of, 159–160
   mistakes made by, 19
   model of, 145–146
   multiple, 99–101
   perfect, 179 (*See also* The
      Black Diamond)
   resilience of, 89, 90
   sample questionnaire for, 204–206
   self-awareness of, 97, 102–103
   social conditioning of, 127–128

solution creations of reasons for
      startups by, 79
   toxic environments created by, 37
      (*See also individual types
      of leaders*)
   unwillingness to learn by, 91–92
   without strong ambition, 86–89
"Founder's dilemma," 159
Founders Taboo, 197–200
Freedom:
   in collectivistic culture, 119
   in individualistic culture, 120–121
Free meals, 27–28
Freeup, 91–92
Frustration, redefinition of self and, 79
Fun, 140, 180

Garton, Eric, 73
Gates, Bill, 79
Generation Y, 10
Genuineness, 162
Gen Z leaders, 7–20
   collateral damage from, 18–19
   and founder culture, 9–10
   learning from, 19–20
   and nepotism, 17
   red flags in paradigm of, 10–16
#Girlboss companies, 146
GitHub, 138
Goal(s):
   CEOs' loss of focus on, 82
   change in, 111–113
   in collectivistic cultures, 118, 132
   in individualistic cultures, 123
   lack of co-creation of, 104–105
   at Revolut, 131
   of startups, 9
"Good leavers":
   because of lack of support, 62
   reasons for resignations by,
      67–71, 75–76

Governance:
around founders, for mental
health, 200
lack of, 17, 19
Green, Carrie, 138
Greensil, 91–92
Groupthink, in collectivistic
culture, 119, 120
Growth:
and change in nature of the
company, 74
importance of community
for, 147–148
loss of founding principles with, 72
need for different people at different
phases of, 190–193
in number of employees, investigat-
ing facts behind, 45–48
and sustaining a healthy
culture, 50–52
Growth mindset, 159–160, 175
Guibaud, Sophie, 182–183

"Hands-off CEOs," 80, 82
Harassment cases, 12–14
Hard news, breaking, 189–190
Hathaway, Ian, 138
Hierarchies:
artificial, 98
in collectivistic culture, 118
early formation of, 72
High performers:
in individualistic cultures, 129–131
resignations by, 107–108 (See also
"Good leavers")
Hiring:
candidates' investigation of founders during, 174
CEO's involvement in, 170–171
by collectivistic founders, 126
of community builders and architects, 139, 143

and companies with lack of ambition, 87–89
in companies without forward
thinking CEOs, 82
and evolution of company, 163
for fast growth, 45–52, 57–58
and forgetting support for
employees, 60–63
to grow community, 156
by individualistic founders, 122–123
inexperienced people's recommendations for, 17
lack of diversity in, 23
under new HR person, 49–50
for the wrong reasons, 59
Hiring plans, 46–47
Hjelm, Fredrik, 141
Honesty, 184
Hopin, 46–48
Human resources (HR):
in companies with satellite
offices, 61
and creation of company culture,
203–204
culture impacted by, 206–207
ignoring professionalism in, 19
new conversation about, 154–155
perspective of, xiv, 5
role of, 10–11, 183–185 (See also
specific HR issues, e.g.: Hiring)
and sharing stories about
ex-employees, 14
size, focus, and output of
teams, 56–58
too-rapid growth of, 72
undervaluing of, 57
working against values in, 20
Hybrid work models, 61

IBM, 26–27
Identity, authentic, 131,
186–188, 193–196

Inclusion:
  company dedicated to conversation
    about, 153
  lack of, 39
Incubators, 79
Individualism. *See also* The
    Collectivist vs. The Individualist
  culture of, 72, 128–131
  misperception of, 125–132
  as opposite of collectivism, 120–125
Influencers:
  founders as, 193
  at heart of communities, 139–140
Infogrid, 165–168
Inquiry, appreciative, 110
Instagram, 138
Integration, 143
Intention(s):
  in creating culture, 179–180
  and impact on others, 195
Investors:
  bringing in people under
    "advice" of, 45
  and mental health needs of
    founders, 200
  pressures from, 144
  and social conditioning of found-
    ers, 127–128
  and startup money, 79–81
  toxic behavior encouraged by, 18
Isenberg, Greg, 144–145

Jackson, Kelly, 118, 183–185
Jenner, Kylie, 79–80
Jobs Steve, 145, 163
Judgment, 110

Karma, 153
The Keen Learner, 157–176
  being vulnerable to forge
    trusts, 164–168

described, 159–160
  as founders vs. as leaders, 175–176
  learning from others, 169–171
  taking feedback and
    support, 161–164
  unwillingness because of
    ego, 172–175
  willingness to learn, 160–161
Kindness, 189
Knowledge map, 161
Kylie Cosmetics, 80

Learning:
  continuous, 206–207
  in corporate job, 3–4
  from experience, 89–91
  founder's unwillingness for, 86, 91–92
  founders who seek (*see* The
    Keen Learner)
  mechanisms of, 161
  from others, 160, 169–171
  in startup industry, 3, 5
  by trailblazers, 97
  willingness for, 89–91, 160–161
Legacy model, breaking, 79
Limiting beliefs, 187
Lincolne, Rob, 90–91
Listening, 207
Luno, 118, 183–185

Management consequences, 13
Managers, founders/CEOs as, 72, 159
Media coverage:
  of startup successes, 23
  of toxic cultures, 39, 40
Mental health, 196
  not addressing issues of, 35
  and psychological burnout, 73
  seeking help in maintain-
    ing, 196–201
  and toxic cultures, 18, 20

Methven, Ross, 98–101
Microaggressions, 196
Micromanagement, 105–109, 168
The Middle Manager, 65–76
  causes of "good leavers,"
    68–71, 75–76
  company factors in people
    leaving, 71–73
  reasons for staying, 73–75
Millennials, 61–62
Mindsets of founders, 159–160, 175
Mission:
  and change of directions, 112–113
  communities with a, 140–144
  early-stage employees' belief in, 76
  extending conversation
    about, 152–155
  failure to align actions and, 150–152
  and "hands-off CEOs," 80
  holding on to, 82–85
  sacrifice of, 87
  values and purpose tied into, 180
  wanting to be part of, 187
Mission-driven approach, 192
Mohanty, Nina, 118–119, 188–190
Murphy, Victoria, 147–150
Musk, Elon, 79

NastyGal, 146
Nepotism, 15–19
Nest Labs, 97–98
Neumann, Adam, 185
N26, 45

Obama, Barack, 189
Office politics, in corporations, 3–4
Onboarding, 50, 72
Ootes, Alex, 122
Opinions, asking for, 190
Oxsed, 88

Passion, 84
Paydock, 89–91
Payhawk, 119
Penfold, Ruth, 193
People leader, role of, 183–185
People management, 56–58
Perfect founders, 179. See also The
    Black Diamond
"Perfect" opportunities, 48–52
Performance cultures, 129–131
Performance measures, 28–33
Perkins, Gillian, 138
Perra, Niccolo, 147–150
Personal financial stress, 201
Personality mapping, 28–30
Personal life, lack of, 26–27
Personio, 141–144, 169–171
Pics, 23
Piddock, Suzanne, 89–91
Pleo, 147–150
Pointer, Tim, 191
Politics, in corporations, 3–4
Psychological burnout, 73
Psychological safety, 180
Purpose:
  clarity of, 188
  commonality of, 180
  consistent commitment to, 101
  culture aligned around, 48
  founder's connection to, 187
  lack of, beyond "get it done," 109

Quora, 138

Ramadani, Merita, 119
Ratner, Miri, 97
Recognition, 72
Relationships, developing, 72
Relationship-like culture, 117–120
Remote work, 61

Renner, Hanno, 142, 169–171
Resignations:
  from companies without
    ambition, 89
  company factors in, 71–73
  compared to hirings, 45
  due to constant change of
    directions, 111–113
  due to not being invested in
    people, 151–152
  of "good leavers," 62, 67–71, 75–76
  and need for company overhaul, 85
  to pursue dreams, 62
  as red flags, 12
  from toxic cultures, 18, 33–35, 39
Resilience, 89, 90, 192
Respect, 188–189
Retention. *See also* Resignations
  employees' reasons for staying, 73–75
  by tenure, 74
Revolut, xiii, 5, 24–35
  Bryan's experience at, 53, 55–56
  community built by, 145
  culture of, 40, 131
  goals at, 131
  hiring process of, 145–146
  learning from, 41
  toxic culture of, 145, 146
Richards, Sam, 141–144
Rindom, Jeppe, 147–150
Ring, 50–53
Rise, 56–58
Risk tolerance, 187
Robles-Anderson, Erica, 145

Safety:
  in building trust, 164
  to fail, lack of, 104
  and sharing of true self, 195
  work environments of, 180, 182–183

Saint Guilhem, Bennis, 172–175
Saint Guilhem, Romain, 172–175
Salaries:
  sacrifice of mission to, 87
  transparency of, 11, 16
Santos, Patricia, 50–53
Satellite offices, 61
Scalability, 9
Self, being true to, 131, 193–196
Self-awareness:
  for authenticity, 187
  balanced with willingness to
    improve, 121
  of founders, 97, 102–103, 172
  of need for mental health help, 197
  openness to, 195
  in shaping identity, 186
Senior management members, 15–16
Shares schemes, 36
Siminoff, Jamie, 51–53
Source Forge, 138
Spanx, 97
Spolsky, Joel, 138
Stack Overflow, 138
Startups, 3–5
  author's perspective on, 5
  born out of Gen Y and Gen Z, 10
  defined, 9
  misconception of, 9
  reasons for creating, 79
  reasons for failure of, 102–103
  resources on, 175
The Startup Community Way
  (Feld and Hathaway), 138
Startup culture, 1, 2, 9. *See also*
  individual companies
Startup money, 79–81.
  See also Investors
Storonsky, Nik, 26, 28–34, 40
Storytelling, 172
Stranex, Timothy, 118

Strategies:
   dearth of updates on, 101
   lack of co-creation of, 104–105
Success of startups:
   and autonomy for employees, 98
   and dialogue around mental
      health, 201
   with low-ego founders, 174–175
   media coverage of, 23
   reliance on community for,
      137, 155–156
   of Talent Acquirers, 53–56
   time as enemy to, 168
Supercharger Ventures, 197
Support:
   of employees, 60–63, 118
   for founder, team in place for, 181
   founder's willingness to
      take, 161–164
   on path to self-awareness, 195
Swanepoel, Marcus, 118, 184

The Talent Acquirer, 43–63
   decision-making by, 58–59
   fast growth under, 45–48
   lack of support for people
      hired by, 60–63
   people management under, 56–58
   and "perfect" opportunities, 48–52
   success patterns of, 53–56
Tamayo, Teresa, 153
Taylor, Simon, 100
Team(s):
   in communities, 140
   complementary, 180–183
   diversity of, 100
   empowering, 71
   helping founders understand
      journey as a, 183–184
   People/HR, 183–185

Tenure, retention by, 74
TikTok, 138
Time:
   as enemy to success, 168
   struggling with, 188
Tinder, 140
Togetherness, culture of, 148
Tone, setting the, 185, 188, 189
Too Good To Go, 153
Toxic cultures/work environments.
      See also individual companies
      and types of leaders
   blame for, 195–196
   creating environments
      opposite to, 37–38
   ego as common denominator
      in, 172
   and ego-based behavior, 102–103
   founder's role in avoiding, 168
   in individualistic culture, 121–124
   managers' lack of control
      over, 71–72
   reasons for creating, 37
   and self-awareness of founders, 97
The Trailblazer, 95–113
   attractions for, 97–101
   blame culture and judgment
      created by, 110
   and confusion from constant
      change of directions, 111–113
   and lack of co-creation of strate-
      gies, 104–105
   and lack of purpose beyond "get it
      done," 109
   and lack of safety to fail, 104
   micromanagement by, 105–109
   reasons for failure of, 102–104
Transparency:
   about mental health needs, 200
   balancing human element
      and, 166–167

in communities, 140
and consistent commitment to
    purpose, 101
culture of, 47
feedback in building culture
    of, 161–163
with loss of focus on founding
    principles, 72
and trust-building, 165
Trust:
    in collectivistic cultures, 132
    people CEOs can trust, 181
    vulnerability in forging, 164–168
Trust-mistrust cycle, 73
The Type A, 21–41
    demands of, 28–30
    intolerance of, 30–33
    learning from, 36–41
    leaving, 33–35
    recruitment of other Type
        As by, 24–28

Uber, 18, 45
The Unlearner, 77–93
    company overhauls, 85–86
    examples of, 79–80
    founder's unwillingness to
        learn, 86, 91–92
    holding on to critical mission,
        82–85
    lack of forward thinking, 81–82
    willingness to learn from experi-
        ence, 89–91
    without strong ambition, 86–89
Unleashed, 154–155

Values:
    clarity of, 188
    in collectivistic cultures, 132

commonality of, 180
embedded, 181
founders as representatives of, 182
founder's connection to, 187
standing for, 207
working against your, 20
Valuing people, 189–190
Visibility, with loss of focus on
    founding principles, 72
Vision:
    being able to build vs., 108–109
    as best chance for startups, 181
    clarity of, 188
    of founders, 9
Voi, 140–141
Voices, in decision-making, 10
Vulnerability:
    accepting, 180
    to forge trusts, 164–168

Well-being, state of, see Mental health
Wework, 185
Wins, celebrating, 189–190
Wired, 150
Women in Tech community, 153
Work environments. See also
    Culture(s); individual
    companies
    communal, 128–132
    and consistent commitment to
        purpose, 101
    desirable, 180
    differing perceptions of, 194–196
    managers' lack of control
        over, 71–72
    non-toxic, creating, 37–38
    safety of, 182–183
    toxic (see Toxic cultures/work
        environments)
    unique to startups, 182

Working hours, extended, 25–28
W Startup Community, 153

Yayar, 97, 98
Y-Combinators, 160
Yeow, Joo Bee, 165–168

Yi Luo, 191–193
YouTube, 138

Zebra Fuel, 172–175
Zuckerberg, Mark, 79